The Enemy Called Failure

The Enemy Called Failure

ISBN: 978-978-970-725-6
1st Printing -May, 2022 - AD

All correspondence to:
The Author
Kingsley T. Ibanichuka
Email; ibaniking@gmail.com

Published by CHLIDEM MEDIA
Cover design by The Xwit Creatives

Unless otherwise indicated, Bible references are from, Easy English Bible, King James Version, The Message Translation, The Passion Translation, New International Version

FOREWORD

That you failed at something does not make you a failure, it only just means you failed at doing that thing. Do it again if it is something you really desire to do. The story shared in The Enemy called Failure is one that is both interesting and inspiring to read. Most students in the Medical and Dental schools would easily relate with some of the jargons and terminologies used in the book, but I can tell you for free that everyone would benefit from reading this book.

For Parents; so, they can properly guide their children who have attempted something and failed before, for students who are in school, and generally for everyone who seeks to cultivate the right attitude towards failure; either when it comes as a personal encounter or when it comes as the experience of friends and loved ones.

The author shares his personal story of overcoming the failures and the disappointments that stood in the way of achieving his dream of becoming a medical doctor. He discloses the disposition of mind that helped him go through the peculiar challenges at various points of his training and I daresay, come out unscathed. I can easily relate with some of the experiences in the book because I had some personal experiences failing some of my professional examinations in School as a Dental student training to become a Dentist. I know failure at an examination is simply failure at that examination, and that if you can get your act together, you can always overcome that same examination at the next attempt. Failing examinations does not make you a failure in life.

Take your time to read every bit of this book so you can have a proper view of what failure is and not be scared to fail.

When Jesus walked on the earth as a man, He was very successful but ended up as a failure by every human standard. Yes, you read that right. He was killed shamefully after all the many mighty miracles and everything He had done. His life on earth ended tragically.
1 Corinthians 2:8 says "Which none of the princes of this world knew: for had they known it, they would not have crucified the Lord of glory."
The princes of this world thought that crucifying Jesus was a perfect way of announcing that He had failed but they were utterly wrong. That which they called "failure" was what God needed to save the entire human race. God's wisdom may sometimes appear as failure in the eyes of men but if we would only look beyond the present circumstances, we would see that God was only up to something greater in the end.

Dr Eghe Aihie
Deputy Chief Executive Officer,
Christian Medical and Dental Association (CMDA), Nigeria.
Lecturer, Department of Physiology,
University of Benin,
Benin-city, Edo state
Nigeria

ACKNOWLEDGEMENT

To my parents, who never judged me as hopeless, but always welcomed my every valley moment and made sure to walk me through to the mountain top.

To my siblings, with you, failing was another reason to try again. You gave all of you, just so I can discover me.

To my friends, a few before my university days, some during my stay at Madonna University and most as a Uniben student, you accepted my failures and never made me feel less of a human.

To my teachers, those who taught me to walk when my legs could not carry me. You never celebrated my failures, for you it was a shared shame.

To Gloria Ejiliwhebi Eguahon, day or night, you gave your best; and to your team of editors, Ofure Angela Ogbidi and Chioma Joy Eleje, you guys made me fluent.

To the TECF team, headed by Samson Oshomoh, you worked tirelessly to see this book take form. Because of you, the world is one book better.

I love each and every one of you.
Thank you.

DEDICATION

To everyone who has failed at something.

CONTENTS

Foreword	**3**
Acknowledgement	**5**
Dedication	**6**
Contents	**7**
In the beginning	**8**
Once upon a time in Okija	**15**
Translated.	**21**
Startling!	**25**
The Arrest	**30**
Back to base	**37**
A New Beginning	**46**
Great UNIBEN	**52**
The Almighty MBBS Part II	**56**
MBBS PART III: The Faith Dance.	**61**
MBBS PART IV: The Long Night	**71**
The Long Night Continues	**87**
The Break of Dawn	**94**
The Finish Line	**108**
The believer is KING over all circumstances.	**116**
The ultimate failure companion.	**130**
Praise for The Enemy Called Failure	**132**

ἑνα
IN THE BEGINNING

This is not an autobiography, neither is it the story of my life. It is a journey through some of my experiences with failure in my quest for the MBBS degree. I have intentionally left out the names of some of the major players as the purpose of this book is solely to simply share this journey with you; not to make a list of names, and certainly not to lay blame.

It is my belief that no one achieves anything worthwhile without making mistakes along life's road. Actually, failures are just mistakes with expensive price tags, and although they may either be minor, major or even deadly mistakes, we've all had our fair share.

In subsequent pages of this book, as you would see; I have documented a few of mine.

I am the last child in a family of ten. We are Christians and hail from the southern part of Nigeria. I had my first attempt at gaining admission into the university in the year 2004. As it is with Nigerian universities, I had to sit for the Joint Admission Matriculation Board (JAMB) examination. Following a long period of soul searching and reality checks, I'd decided that my preferred course of choice was Medicine and Surgery. I remember the day I had that discussion with my dad and the subsequent excitement it brought to my family- the prospect of having a medical practitioner in the family. So, I purchased the form for the exam, and set out to prepare for it. This I did by enrolling in extramural classes to help sharpen and broaden my understanding in The Use of English, Biology, Physics and Chemistry; the subjects that aspiring candidates were required to pass, in order to be considered by the board for admission into medicine.

Aspiring candidates also had the option of choosing two universities and two courses of study as their first and second choices respectively. Majority of my peers desired to migrate from their state of residence to study in universities in distant locations, perhaps to finally be independent and free from the suffocating supervision of their parents and guardians. However, the university of Port-Harcourt (UNIPORT), which is a federal university, was all I wanted. I do not now know if this desire could be attributed to the stories my older siblings had shared from their own earlier adventures in the said school, peer pressure from a few friends who wanted the same thing, or perhaps I was just being a "Port-Harcourt boy". Anyways, she'd stolen my heart, so much so that I chose her as my first and second choices of institution, and Medicine as my first and second choices of course of study.

The day of the exam came with all the accompanying stories and a roller-coaster of emotions. I'd heard about JAMB: the hassles, the fear of failing the exam which meant another terrifyingly long year at home, invigilators shouting at the top of their voices to control the candidates who were all high on adrenaline. There was also this array of Security men outside the hall chasing relatives, friends, well-wishers and even criminals to stay far from the examination hall.

After I'd written the exam, the next thing was the anxiety that marked the days preceding the release of the results. Finally, the results were released as announced in the local news headlines. It quickly became the word on the street as everyone knew someone who took the examination. The journey to the JAMB office to check my results was nothing short of a nerve-racking experience; I could feel the heaving asynchronous rhythm in my chest, my palms were sweaty and my mind was racing through all the possibilities that could arise. Failing meant having to wait an extra year to re-sit the exams on one hand, and on the other hand, scoring below the cutoff mark for medicine meant admission into another course.

After making it to JAMB office early that fateful morning and pushing my way through the mammoth crowd of 'hopefuls' who were on ground to either check their result or that of someone else, I eventually submitted my JAMB registration paper, which I'd carefully kept, to the attendant. A couple of minutes later, I was given the verdict that all the results for my examination center had been withheld. This meant that all candidates who had written in the same center I did, had advertently been denied their result for that year, and this usually happened when the examinations in the said center were fraught with malpractice or irregularities that suggested same.

To say the least, this news left me devastated. My feet felt like lead as I slowly trudged home with a million thoughts of what might have gone wrong plaguing my mind and the dilemma of how I would eventually break the news that I'd be spending the next year at home and not at the university to my family. Like most young secondary school leavers and youths my age, I pretty much had the trajectory of my life all mapped out: by age twenty-seven, I was to be done with my education, saving lives as a wealthy surgeon and married to a beautiful damsel with at least a kid. Alas, my dreams seemed like a castle in thin air with the current reality.

With grief in my heart, I informed my family of what had happened and actually expected the heavens to fall. However, as disappointed as they were with the outcome of my exams (I mean, what Nigerian parent wouldn't want their child gaining admission into the higher institution immediately after secondary school?), I was encouraged to prepare for the next exam. "You are still young and can take the next JAMB and still make it out as a doctor in record time"; everyone said. And although in Nigeria, medicine and surgery is a six-year course on paper, it's actually within seven to ten years in reality. Reasons for this delay are not far-fetched - ranging from academic strikes from the Academic Staff Union of Universities (ASUU) over unending and protracted issues with the Federal Government, to schools losing part or full accreditation to offer medicine as a program me; and their students having to wait till it is regained. In some cases, for some unknown reasons, the medical program would just be extended.

With the unflinching support of my family, I dusted off the recent blow, and looked away from the fact that I would not be going to the University that year. My friends who passed their JAMB examination moved on, and I had to settle for trying again the following year.

The period between my first and forthcoming JAMB examination was filled with questions. Everyone wanted to know my score and what school gave me admission. My answer was simple; my result was withheld. The wait for the next exam was over sooner than I expected and the drill for the next was pressing again. The cycle of going to the library in the morning, waking up at night to read, and extramural classes, was on again. This time, I had learnt from my mistakes and was willing to go the extra mile in order to ace the exam. The D-day came and I wrote the exam once again. I went through the waiting period; expectations were high, in the hopes that affliction would not arise the second time. When the result came out, I didn't hesitate to check for my result within the first week of release. To say the least, I was very anxious. Eventually, I checked the result and the outcome was the same as the last; no result again—*candidate's result withheld.*

The interpretation was as clear as day: yet another year at home, another year to be tagged 'the dumb kid on the block', or should I say, "The unlucky kid". The dream to graduate and be married with kids by 27 years just received another extension by a year. At this point, I was desperate. I wanted anything, as long as it was going to point to medicine and surgery, to occupy me academically in the confines of the university community.

If only I had a JAMB score, things would have been different. Even if it was not up to the cut-off mark required to give me admission into medicine, I was willing to apply for a pre-degree program. However, this was far from my reality. I remember telling my dad I wanted to travel as far as Kwara state for an A-level program that was capable of fetching me admission into 200 Level if I came out with top grades. The manner in which my dad dismissed it, made me believe he did not even give it a thought. Parents though; maybe he could not see his boy travel that far away from home for an A-Level course.

Again, I was encouraged to take the next JAMB. This would be my third trial, three years on the line. My friends with whom I had started the race with and who had gained admission with the first attempt at the exam; were well on their way to 300 Level. I registered for the third JAMB, resolute not to change either choice of school or course of study. It was Medicine and Surgery all the way. The concern of how old I would be when I would finally graduate was beginning to find a place in my mind, but I wanted medicine so badly that I did not think too much about that.

Somewhere between leaving secondary school and my third attempt at JAMB,

I became an apprentice at JEWEL TEC- a goldsmith shop situated in the Judiciary Quarters where we resided at the time. Asides giving me my earliest paycheck, this shop served as a mold for me. It was more than a shop; it was a school out of school. I learnt a lot about the way life works, the way the human mind works and the power it holds. We had a compact disc player with which we listened daily to different players in business, inspirational speakers and content creators. No genre of music was missing from the office collection. We read books that made us understand the power a man wielded over his own destiny. Materials that taught me even then that failure was not the end for those who desired to win big; all thanks to my boss back then.

Around the same period, my elder brother also introduced me to the art and invaluable habit of reading books. I remember that he gave me books like 'Alexander the great', 'Richest man in Babylon', '48 Laws of power'. Armed with numerous stories of conquerors, liberators and tyrants, my mind was open to the big picture about life.

My foundation as a Christian would later be a reason to reject some of the principles in some of these books, as they go against core Christian values. All the same, this period of my life was a major factor in deciding the kind of person I am today. I will say it was a critical point in my life, and I thank God it added value to my life.

When they released the result for my third JAMB exam, everyone in my family was tired of me staying at home for the same reason- result withheld. Yes, my result was withheld for the third time in a row. In fact, this time around, all the results from the center where I wrote were withheld. Devastated is an understatement of how I felt. At this point, we were desperate for a way out.

Failure Tonic 1

Failure is not meant to stop you but to empower you to do more.

A bend on the road is not the end, and it can only be if the bend is your destination.

On your way to your destination, while on a bus, you most likely would encounter many stops. The bus stops to either drop off or receive other passengers. You don't jump down just because it is a bus stop. You stay put until it gets to your destination. Failing at a task is like getting to the bus stop which is not yours. You keep at it till you arrive at your destination.

If the right attitude to failing is put forth, one learns from the mistake and makes amends towards victory. Learning from your errors empowers you to do more and do right.

δύο

ONCE UPON A TIME IN OKIJA

As a child I fancied studying medicine abroad. And in my quest, I had attended some specially organized seminars on gaining admission into foreign universities. I had also written SAT, with my eyes on TOEFL.

My dad was pretty hell-bent on ensuring that I didn't spend another year at home. After going through several possible options as appropriate for my peculiar case of not having a JAMB result, we eventually settled for Madonna University, Okija. The plan was to go through their pre-degree program for medicine, and if I was successful, I would use it as a route to gaining admission into the degree programme of Medicine and Surgery. This would require hard-work, which I was more than ready to do.

Madonna University is the first catholic university in Nigeria. It has three campuses across the country: the Okija campus in Anambra State where the university began in 1999, the Akpugo campus in Enugu State, and the Elele campus in Rivers State; which became the main campus in 2004, and which would eventually become my campus. The campuses had different faculties and departments. However, Madonna University is one hundred percent run like a boarding school.

The first time I heard about Madonna University was a few years earlier when one of my elder brothers received an admission letter from the institution to study Accounting. Although He did not apply to Madonna, the admission letter came through JAMB. He did not accept the admission, and this was because his choice was my State-owned university.

With the consensus being Madonna, my elder brother and I set out to visit the Okija campus in Anambra State to make firsthand enquiries and to process my admission. I had never travelled that far before then. I remember when our vehicle drove past the Elele campus on our way to the Okija. I screamed to my brother as a matter of urgency- *"see am". I* felt we had passed the school and the driver needed to stop. My brother and the passenger next to us laughed and explained to me that it was the Elele campus and our journey was to the Okija campus. It was a very long ride for me; but one I was willing to take.

We arrived the Okija campus that same day, located the administrative block, made the necessary enquiries and proceeded with meeting the admission requirements. Long story short, I was given the admission and was to resume my pre-degree programme at the Elele campus where Medicine and Surgery was offered. This was in July 2006, and after three years and three attempts at JAMB with no result, I was about to commence my higher education studies in a private university. This was far from anything I had dreamt of. The only hope I held on to was that it was another route to standing a chance at getting admitted into medicine.

In July 2006, I became a Madonna University student, and the goal was clear—to gain admission into the degree program to study Medicine and Surgery, although the University of Port Harcourt had always been my dream school. Unfortunately, I could not gain admission there; if only any of my JAMB results were released, even if the score did not meet the requirement for medicine, if it was at least 200, I knew I would have been able to apply for the pre-degree program in UNIPORT, known generally as 'Basic'. I knew how tough Basic was, because at the end of the program, only a select few got admitted into medicine. So, here I was in Madonna University's pre-degree program, an equivalent of UNIPORT's *Basic*, and I was ready for the fight.

To me, this was my ticket to my dream course, and I got to leave the house like my mates in the university. Now, I could enjoy university breaks and harvest stories to tell when I visited home, and among friends.

Regarding Madonna University, there were a lot of stories about the rules governing the school. All these I heard for the first time when I was already admitted. Many were not what should ideally be found in an institution of higher learning if students were really to be properly groomed in knowledge and character and at the same time not robbed of their voices. I believe university students should be allowed to make guided choices, and if they fail; to get up and correct their mistakes. But like a few other students, I made up my mind to abide with the rules and regulations of the school. Basically, if one had decided to be a Madonna University student then you had agreed to live by the rules that governed the school, no matter how absurd. That said, this book is neither about Madonna University nor is it really about my experiences there, but about my experiences with failure as I journeyed towards MBBS. For this reason, I have deliberately kept the spotlight on myself.

The fees were high and nothing close to what was obtainable in a government-owned institution, but my family was ready to do all in their power to see me move on with my dreams. Fees were paid, hopes were high, and expectations were certainly up the roof. As days went by, I found myself some awesome friends in the pre-degree and degree programs, ranging from medical to non-medical students. Most importantly, I found myself a family in the Pentecostal fellowship.

Madonna University; being a catholic school, allowed only one group for non-Catholics - the Pentecostal Fellowship of Madonna (PFM). Regardless of your creed or affiliations, if you were not a catholic and didn't want to attend the Catholic Church, your only option was PFM.

It was home and sanity for many students, and was characterized by the usual intensity and activities common to the Pentecostals. Run by students, one could very much expect all the *razzmatazz* students conjured. They had different groups or units, most of which we find in our home churches—prayer band, ushers, sanctuary keepers—you'd love those guys; to some they appeared unspiritual, maybe because they did their job with a lot of fun, zeal and muscle. And then, there was also the welfare unit, which I later became a part of and gave my heart to. It became home to me. We took care of the welfare of the members of the fellowship, including the leaders. We bonded so well, and we did our job with cheerfulness and excitement. I made good friends in whom I found brothers and sisters; most I am in touch with till date.

Eventually, the end of the Pre-degree came, and I successfully made it to first year medicine. Soon our matriculation numbers reflected our new status; mine was MD/06/646. The joy at home was more than I can describe. Finally, I was a bonafide medical student. The longtime dream to become a medical doctor was back on track. Once again, I made up my mind to be dedicated to my studies, to give it all it took. Classes went on as they should, and in-courses came with the regular tension seen among medical students.

At long last, I was living my dream.

Failure Tonic 2

Failure tests our resolve to achieve the desired goal.

Each time we miss the target, it is as though failure is screaming out to us with a mock grin-"Let me see how badly you want this." How will you respond to this question? With your tail between your legs as you run away? Or you will stand up tall, and walk the talk? We must respond adequately if we truly want to achieve our goals. We must look failure straight in the eye and scream back, "Just one more, 'til I'm done!"

Yes, you'll give it another go till you achieve the desired target.

TRANSLATED.

I am from a devout Christian home. We are Anglicans and attend St. Cyprian Anglican church in Port Harcourt, called famously, 'The Cathedral on land'. My father is a Lay reader and a member of many units in the church, and two which stand out for me are the missions and evangelism group; whose core activities involved travelling to villages to preach the gospel of Jesus Christ. I remember one instance where they went to a village highly renowned for its practice of witchcraft. When my father and the rest of the team shared the tales about the village, it was literally a dark place to my ears, I was scared something bad would happen to them.

The other group was the prayer band. This was the fire and power house of the church. My mum was a dedicated and committed member of this group. I was privileged to attend prayer meetings with them, as well as the Wednesday prayer and fasting meetings for which my mum was impressively consistent. These meetings shaped my youth.

My home is like any other typical Christian home: we had morning devotions daily around 5:30am. Over the years, the kick off time for devotion became 5:00am, and currently begins at 4:30am. The reason for the adjustment in time could not be more explicit than this: as my parents got older, they slept less and woke up earlier. The other reason can be ascribed to the fact that for us the children, as we grew up and had to go about our business of the day, praying early would allow enough time to prepare for the day after the prayers.

I said all this to point to my Christian background, and that I was familiar with the church and religion generally. My association with PFM made me see that there was more to being a Christian than just being a church member and being conversant with Christian rituals. I knew I had to accept the life that Jesus gives. I needed to be saved, to be born again. So, sometime around September 2008, I went early to my lecture hall (I fancy myself an early bird). Right there in my class, I prayed and accepted the life that Jesus gives, acknowledged his saving power and lordship over me. I was born again, translated from the power of darkness to the kingdom of light. Immediately, I picked my phone and sent text messages to everyone in my family that I was born again. I cannot really tell what made me do that, I just felt I should let everyone know about my new life in Christ.

Studying medicine anywhere in the world is difficult. The work load is daunting. And in a Nigerian University, it is even tougher, I think. The learning environment is almost always toxic and depressing to the average medical student. Lecturers who inspire you are quite a handful, while the ones who put you down are everywhere. More so, studying medicine in Madonna University was harder than the regular university. During my time there, the school lacked the required accreditation to graduate her maiden set, and this led to backlog of students. In medical schools with accreditation issues, it is common to see more than one Level existing at the same time; 300 Level A, 300 Level B, 400 Level A, B and C. This was the case with Madonna University then.

In 2009, I was in 300 Level. Anyone who is familiar with the medical school program knows that this level is the first real test of your resilience. In 300 Level, you get to write your first professional examination, the second MB.BS (Bachelor of Medicine and Bachelor of Surgery). In some schools, it is called first MB.BS. The student is required to pass courses in basic medical sciences; Anatomy, Biochemistry and Physiology.

Aside from these basic courses, some schools might be engaged with community health, as was the case in Madonna. You didn't get to write community health examination in 300 Level till final year, but you took the lectures and wrote tests along the way.

Failure Tonic 3

There is nothing wrong in failure; it is as right as success.

We have been taught to celebrate successful people, and ridicule those who fail. “Success is good, and failure is bad”, they say. Success must be embraced and failure avoided like a deadly contagious disease.

A close study of success would reveal that failure is almost at the other side of success. Just learn to flip the coin to the other side. The moment you fail, know this for sure: success is at the door. The line between winning and losing can be so thin we miss it: like flipping the head of the coin to reveal the tail.

Τέσσερα

STARTLING!

Towards the end of 2009, the heat for our first professional exam was intense, as the examination was scheduled for early 2010. Almost every lecturer from the Basic Medical School was preparing us for one in-course or another that would count towards our first professional exam. Around the same time, our community health lecturer decided to take us on a week-long marathon of lectures. This was certainly inconveniencing to all of my classmates. Now, the class was not compulsory but optional. A lot of my colleagues ditched the classes, and a handful of us attended, not because it was convenient, but simply because we didn't want to miss out on the lecture. Literally, students attended the class grumbling, as we had to stay in class from morning till about 3:00pm to 4:00pm daily, with a short break around midday.

Another reason why I attended was because of my relationship with this Community Health lecturer. I saw him as one of my favorite lecturers because of his humane and Christian disposition to students. In fact, there was this one time I nursed the desire to do research, and find an alternative to the use of formaldehyde (formalin) used in preserving cadaver for medical students. Formalin is very irritating, as it caused our eyes and nose to tear and run uncontrollably, it also caused the throat to itch and this made dissections for pre-clinical students very uncomfortable. So, I said to myself- 'why not find out an alternative option?'

I then decided to carry out research on the preservation of cadavers in other countries. I needed a guide, and the one person I could go to was my Community Health lecturer, and he was very helpful and friendly. Now, I'm sure you understand when I say I attended the classes because of my good relationship and rapport with him.

In one of those classes; seeing how tired we looked, the lecturer asked if we had anything to say as regards the classes, and initially, nobody in the class responded. This was surprising because outside the classroom my classmates complained endlessly about the burden of juggling the marathon of classes and preparation for the many in-courses lined up towards the second MBBS examination, and how it was wrongly timed. Finally, we were being given the opportunity to air our displeasure, but no one wanted to say anything.

I raised my hand and thanked the lecturer for the classes and the opportunity to make a comment, I then went ahead to tell him of the stress we were going through, trying to meet up with examination requirements and his classes, and of the fact that we spend almost all our productive hours in this marathon of classes, and when we left the class, we were so tired we could barely do anything else but sleep and repeat the cycle the following day. And on the second point he had made before regarding how we didn't read enough, and didn't go to the library to research on the topics taught. I wondered aloud how we could do this if we spent the whole day in class with little or no time to engage in other academic important pursuits.

When I said this, the lecturer was taken aback and was not happy with the class. He berated the class for not saying anything about the stress the classes were putting us through. At this time, every other person started speaking up. He gave us listening ears and eventually, he proposed we just bear with him for a day or two, and allow him wrap up so we could give all the attention to preparations for our in-courses. We agreed and set out to give the last push to end the marathon. Everyone was happy, it seemed. This was a democratic win, but unknowingly; the beginning of the spiraling black hole for my dreams of bagging an MBBS degree from Madonna University.

We were to wrap up the series of lectures with a seminar in Community Health. As we planned and prepared for this, shocking news surfaced, one that was quite sad and unnecessary. Our Community Health lecturer announced that he received a text message from an anonymous fellow threatening him not to go on with the seminar, or else he and his children would be kidnapped. The sender accused the lecturer of trying to use the seminar as an avenue to give marks to his favorite students.

This move by the sender, maybe a joke, probably intended to stop the seminar, as he or she perhaps was afraid of flunking it. But I believed then as I do now that it was too expensive and highly unnecessary.

The lecturer promised the class that if the student owned up; he would forgive and let it go. No one owned up. No words in or outside the class pointed to anyone, at least none that I heard. The issue died down; the lecturer had forgiven whoever the sender was and allowed ‘vengeance to be served by God’, in his words.

Soon, it was December and the countdown for Christmas break began. The joy of seeing my family again; a breath of fresh air. Christmas in my home is always beautiful as everyone comes back home from within and outside the State. Friends and relatives get to visit our house, and we find time to visit theirs too. For me that attended a 'boarding' University, I got to catch up with a lot that happened while I was not around.

Oh, the Christmas hymns in church, the splendor of St. Cyprian Anglican church: all priceless. In all of these, one thing was constant, and that was the plenty food to go around.

Failure Tonic 4

Why fear failure when it leads to success?

If you are told that failure leads to success, would you still dread the prospect of failing? I doubt it. However, every successful person knows this truth. It is an open secret appreciated by only those who truly want to achieve their desires. The more they fail, the closer they get to their dreams. So, no matter how much they fail, they keep trying again with new ideas till they succeed.

πέντε

THE ARREST

In January 2010, I was set for school, and the goal for the year was to smash my second MBBS. It was a common sight for some students to either resume late or forfeit their admission, and it's usually because they had gotten transferred to other universities, relocated abroad or just blatantly refused to come back to Madonna University. They would rather stay at home than face the rules that hit like being an inmate in a maximum-security prison.

I'd made up my mind long ago, that no matter the heat I received in the school; I was to leave there with my MBBS degree. I adjusted my expectations of a university to fit into what was available in Madonna. I had come this far, and the next phase was to pass my second MBBS. I was not the best in my class, but I was very sure I would pass my exams.

While everyone was still relishing the scent and pleasures at home, still trying to psyche themselves into the whole back-to-school mode and ready to be students in the confines of Madonna walls for another semester, we heard in class that one of our classmates had been picked by the school's Security team in connection to the threat sent to our lecturer the previous year. The arrest of this fellow was only the first of the four made in the hours that followed.

I was still trying to process my thoughts around the sudden turn of events when I was arrested by the Security team later that day. I was dazed, in shock the whole period. I could not believe my eyes and what was happening. I tried reaching the lecturer to come to our rescue, at least to come and speak to the security that I was not liable to carry out such an act but all my efforts were to no avail. That night, I was not allowed to go back to my hostel, and was forced to spend the night at the corridor of the Security post. And as the custom was, the school's security outfit dubbed "G-Unit" had packed my belongings from my room to the security post. A few of my friends came visiting to know what was happening and what they were to do to help my plight. However, they met the arrogance and sheer inhumanity of the G-Unit staff who chased them away. As they left me that night, I felt alone and really pitied myself. Tears rolled down my cheeks as I watched them leave, utterly distraught at how I found myself in such a mess. I remembered my mother had called me at about the same period of the arrest, and I could not take her call, I guess her motherly instincts brought me to her mind at that moment and she wanted to hear from me and find out if I was alright. The pain cut deep with the thought of my parents getting to know about this. I had done everything; from adjusting to the rules and regulations in Madonna to practically living daily as a kindergarten student, just to stay out of trouble.

In the morning, my friends returned to check on me alongside some fellowship members including members of the welfare unit of PFM. We were asked to write statements for the events for which we had been apprehended, and were let go of, after many arguments and highly derogatory remarks from the security men. If I chose to describe the ineptitude and stark unprofessionalism of these security men, I would be deviating from the story line and would take the focus away from me, which I had earlier stated was the goal of this book.

Between January 2010 and February 2010, the school set up a panel made up of the Chief Security Officer, the Dean of Students, Deputy Registrar and other staff, to investigate and come to a verdict on which of us sent the text message to our lecturer. I remember one of the days, before one of the panel meetings; I had gone to the lecturer in question and pleaded with him to come and narrate to the panel what happened that day in class- how it was just an innocent conversation between a group of students and their lecturer and how it ended. He said he would not be around as he had somewhere else to be in. I could not imagine him being absent from a trial that was centered on him. He ended up sending a hand-written statement and continued with his journey.

By this time, my family was fully aware, and my dad, two of my eldest siblings and my cousin had paid a visit to the school to know the charges against me. The Chief Security Officer, a fair, huge man, with a strong Igbo accent; wasted no time in telling them how I challenged my lecturer in class and instigated other students to do same and for that reason, was the prime suspect for that threat made by text to my lecturer. My Dad tried to convince him of my innocence and integrity, but all that he had to say fell on deaf ears. They left that day and returned subsequently on other visits to face the same back-and-forth arguments. Many times, they were met with the pompousness of the Chief Security Officer and his men, and on other occasions, the same people would be warm to my Dad and respond like a way out had been found already.

In one of the panel's sessions, I was questioned on my interactions in class that day. I narrated the whole issue again to them as I'd done severally to anyone who cared to listen. The panel questioned me about the text message and

I explained how like every other classmate, I had come to hear about it. I said to them, "Why would I send a text message to threaten my lecturer, preventing him from organizing the seminar, when I attended all the lectures and was one of the class members that reached an agreement with the lecturer on how to conclude the lectures and have the seminar to round off the marathon, so we could go and prepare for our in-course?"

In fact, if there was any student to be called the lecturer's favorite, I counted myself one because of our cordial relationship. They hardly paid attention to what I was saying. They were bent on associating the event from the class with the text message. They spoke and acted as people who had arrived at a conclusion already. I remembered one of the panel members telling me in a session that they would *throw away the baby and the water* if we would not own up.

From the day of the first arrest in January down to February, I went through hell. My baggage; including my clothes and essential belongings, was still in the custody of the school security. I had to make do with the few clothes left with me as I tried to prepare for my second MBBS examination which was scheduled for the following month. As you would imagine, it was difficult, because right before my eyes, my dreams and hard work were about to be washed down the drain. I'd spent few months short of four years of my life chasing this dream of mine. I spent days praying and believing that this whole nightmare would come to an end so I could go back to being a normal student again. I was confident God would see me through, and everyone that was aware was praying for me.

On the 18th of February, we received the verdict of the panel. They had arrived at a conclusion after weeks of making no headway as to finding out who actually sent the text message to the lecturer. This was their conclusion as contained in the letter they gave to me:

"Madonna University does not condone any unwholesome activity and behavior. Series of investigations and evidence before the students' disciplinary committee revealed that: you manifested an unwholesome behavior by standing up and informing your lecturer that he was wasting everyone's time, while he informed the class of a seminar. By your unwholesome behavior, you instigated other members of your class to lose interest in the lecturer's proposed seminar.

After due interrogations and following the evidence adduced, you admitted before the disciplinary committee that you were guilty of the offences.

These actions of yours negate the rules and regulations of this noble University which you signed to uphold at the time you were admitted into the institution.

The University authority consequently has decided to suspend you indefinitely from the University.

You are therefore hereby suspended indefinitely with immediate effect.

You are to submit to the authority your student ID card and any other Madonna University property in your possession. Furthermore, you are to leave the University vicinity immediately in your own interest.

This was a very sad day for me and for everything I had looked forward to. I could not wrap my head around what had just happened. Before we could say jack, the school security van took us to the hostel, evacuated our remaining belongings and bundled us out of the school and offloaded us at the Elele motor park. Four of us, too bewildered to do anything, stood and watched the van take off back to school without us. It was devastating to see how the whole ordeal eventually ended: I never saw it coming. Where would I start from? What would I tell my family? What would their responses be? After all these years, the huge school fees paid, the sacrifices made by my family for me to afford to pay all that a private school demanded, all these down the drain, just a waste! Somehow, we boarded vehicles to our different directions. I went back to my home in Port Harcourt: back to my family, back to the beginning.

Failure Tonic 5

Those who have high tolerance for failure inevitably succeed.

I am convinced that all those who learn from their failures, no matter how many times they end up failing, will succeed. Tolerating failure doesn't make you a failure. It shows you know that failure means no harm but teaches a lesson that maybe, success may never teach.

BACK TO BASE

At home, it was heart breaking to see how my parents and siblings felt. It was a setback and a dark moment for us. While we sobbed, we also wondered what the way forward would be. I must say that at this time, it was as if another spirit had come upon me, for my confidence and trust in God grew with each passing day. One thing I knew was responsible for my strength was the word of God. With every opportunity, I was listening to Pastors Chris Ugoh of Kings Assembly, Nkechi Ene of The Carpenter's Church, and Ugochukwu Unachukwu of Recovery House Church. I was so hopeful that when some of my friends from school called me to console me, some crying and others barely able to speak; even though they called with the intention of encouraging me, I ended up comforting them. They called in, sad and down, but ended the call on a high note. I assured them I was going to come back to school. I had prayed, and my father would be coming to see the school management for a way out, since it was an indefinite suspension and not an expulsion.

I kept on reading at home for my second MBBS, constantly calling my friends at school to know what was taught each day, so as to align my own study plan. My hopes were pretty high that I would be back in school just in time for the exam. When the exams did not hold in March, and I was not back in school yet, I thanked God for the delay and believed it was all working for my good.

My dad sprang to action and started the journey to Madonna to discuss a way out. Each day he went, I would call up my friends in school to guide him through the offices. He met with the Chief Security Officer whose responses to him were as fluctuating as his emotions for the day was; favorable with a way out for good some days, and other days, fire and brimstone. My dad met other principal officers to seek a way out. And eventually, he was told only the chancellor could revoke the decision, reverse the indefinite suspension and call me back to school. His attention thereafter shifted to seeing the Chancellor, which was not easy as hundreds of catholic faithfuls and non-Catholics with one issue or the other, physical or spiritual, all requested an audience with him. Not to talk of the many foreigners who came to see for themselves the rumors they'd heard about Madonna. And so, seeing the Chancellor was a herculean task. You'd have to join the queue, sometimes for days. My dad went every day in order to see the Chancellor.

On the 22nd of March 2010, my dad met with the Chancellor in his office and narrated the whole matter to him, and the Chancellor directed him to go put his appeal in writing and come back to see him. What glimpse of hope this birthed at home and amongst my friends for the way out was finally here.

Or so we thought.

The next day, my dad wrote the first letter in appeal for my reinstatement:

Application for re-instatement from suspension of Mr. Ibanichuka Tamunoala, K

I hereby refer to my meeting with you in your office on Monday, 22nd March, 2010 and your directive to me that I should apply for the re-instatement from indefinite suspension of Mr. Tamunoala K. Ibanichuka, a level 300 student in the faculty of medicine and surgery, in your university.

I have to remind you, dear Father, that in your office, I told you that I have a burden in my heart and I believe Christ will relieve me through you.

Tamunoala is my last child, and I am now a pensioner. A setback in his academic progress shall be a stress to my health and financial position. I hereby humbly beg you father, to reconsider the suspension with mercy.

I am ready to enter into any bond together with my son, and I believe by the grace of God, we shall keep it. A copy of the letter for indefinite suspension is attached herein.

May the good Lord bless you and your future aspirations.

The letter was submitted as agreed. It seemed the end of the suspension was here, but this thought in itself soon proved to be a delusion as my father had to visit Madonna again and again just to get the verdict from the Chancellor. Days turned into weeks, weeks into months. In the space of one year, my father tried to reach the Chancellor to no avail. Some days, with my siblings and cousins, but many times he went alone. Every day he left the house, we prayed and hoped that day would be fruitful. Looking back, I can only imagine the weight my parents had to bear, each day my dad came back from Madonna. I say this because I know parents keep a certain degree of their pain from their children.

Most of those visits to see the chancellor spanned from as early as 6:00am-8:30am to 5:00pm, and before my dad would get home, it would be around 7:00pm-8:00pm. On many occasions, he came back home too tired to even eat and just went straight to bed. Some days, my dad and the other visitors would be asked to carry blocks from where they were stacked, to the building site: the church auditorium in Elele campus was very much under construction in those days.

As at March 2011, there had been no change to the status quo. By this time, my dad already had some interactions with other principal officers and was advised to write a letter to the Vice Chancellor, which he did.

The letter was dated 28th March 2011 and was addressed to the Chancellor of Madonna University.

Further application for re-instatement from indefinite suspension of Mr. Ibanichuka, Tamunoala, K.

I am writing as a further appeal to you, reminding you that my son, Mr. Ibanichuka Tamunoala K, a level 300 student in the faculty of medicine and surgery in your university, given indefinite suspension since 18th February, 2010 be considered for re-instatement.

By your directive, Father, I wrote the first application, dated 23rd March 2010, addressed to you. Copies of the suspension letter and my application are attached herein for your perusal.

Between March, 2010 and March, 2011, I have visited your campus about 22 times, showing my desire that my son continue and finish his course at Madonna

University.

I am beginning to feel the effect of the indefinite suspension which has lasted more than one year. I find it difficult to believe, considering the humble Christian background Tamunoala is born into, that he would have committed such offence. Besides, Tamunoala told me the lecturer it was alleged that he referred the words to, is one of his closest lecturers.

The suspension is unfortunate.

However, I still appeal that it be reconsidered.

Seeking for your help,

I remain,

Yours truly.

This appeal also got no response from the Chancellor and the School management. The silence was traumatizing to my family to say the least. For me, I had an unusual enablement which I totally ascribe to God. My hopes of returning back to Madonna University was so high it could power a city if it was electricity. In 2010, I was advised to take another JAMB but, I was having none of it. I believed I would be called back, and besides, another JAMB would mean starting the journey all over again. A few felt it was time to choose a four-year course.

For many, I was still a student in Madonna University, as I was not always present at home and my response to the question "how is school?" was always "fine". After the indefinite suspension, I spent my time shuttling between Bayelsa and Port Harcourt. Two of my siblings worked and lived in Yenagoa, the capital city of Bayelsa. Yenagoa became a haven for me. It kept me away from the constant piercing gaze and outright questioning from everyone around, as they all knew I attended an "all boarding" school and should not be around. Only a few close friends and my immediate family knew what was truly going on.

As much as I shuttled between Yenagoa and Port Harcourt, I spent most of my time in Yenagoa. This also afforded me the opportunity to stay away from the constant gaze of my dad and mum: they looked upon me with so much sympathy, I literally felt their sorrow; it felt like I was causing them pain. In all these, they never acted bitter or discouraging to me. There was never a time when they made my suspension a reference point in any conversation in order to correct me or admonish me. They constantly encouraged me; my family was very supportive.

This break in academic activities afforded me the time to place emphasis on other things. One of which has helped me grow in a sense of my heritage in Christ was the opportunity to attend Word of Faith Bible Institute (WOFBI). WOFBI is a ministry/leadership training arm of the Living Faith Church. Between late 2010 and 2011, I went through the Basic Certificate Course (BCC), Leadership Certificate Course (LCC) and the Diploma Certificate Course (DCC) at Winners Chapel, Kaduna Street, D-Line, Port Harcourt. This period was life-transforming, and looking back now, I can boldly say, it was God preparing me for the future. Simply put, WOFBI was the beginning of a new world for me, as my eyes were opened to the believer and all his possibilities walking in faith. Again, my courage to face life's uncertainties was empowered. I rose above defeat and discouragement. I was full of hope for life, and my trust in God took a turn upwards. I became so bold with my faith at life's ordeal and challenges. Thank God for those classes and all I learnt;

they were internalized. A word almost every teacher kept repeating at WOFBI was, "WOFBI is not to make pastors out of you but to equip you with the knowledge of your heritage in Christ". True to this, I was equipped for life.

Failure Tonic 6

The family, by extension the home, should be the first place a child is taught that failure is not a death sentence.

How often the child who takes a longer time to learn a thing or maybe does poorly at school is termed a failure and, in many instances, is less appreciated when compared to the kid who is having straight A's.

The home is the first place the child learns about life. If children are taught to try again when they fail, if they are brought to the table and lovingly told that failure is not a death sentence but a lesson teacher, they would learn to see failure for what it is: a friend and not the enemy.

How often are children scared to come back home because they failed at school, and worse still, when a neighbor's child did excellently well. They know shame awaits them at home.

The right teaching would be for the child to run home whenever they fail, because that is where he goes back to strategize on the drawing board to try again.

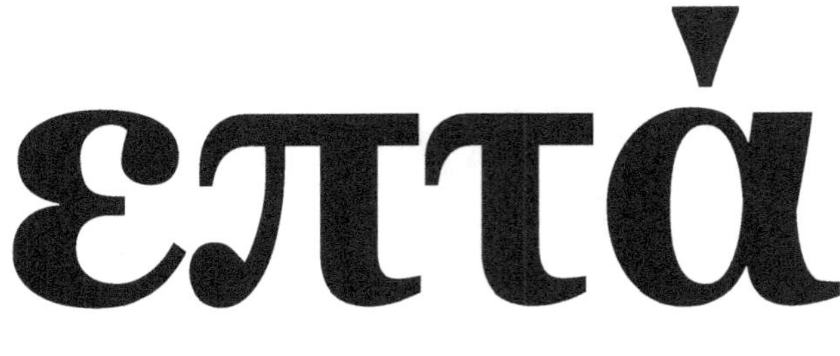

A NEW BEGINNING

In 2012, it was becoming clear that looking away from Madonna University was the ideal thing to do. This was almost two years after the suspension and not a single word from Madonna University: not even a rejection of our appeals and numerous visits. My Dad's visits gradually reduced, and I eventually agreed to sit for another JAMB examination. Only this time, the zeal with which I wrote the first had massively suffered a huge blow, as I noticed the drag to read as I ought to. Nevertheless, I read and prepared for the examination. This time, I made a change in my choice of institution and chose the prestigious University of Benin (UNIBEN). Growing up, in my subconscious, I had a little desire, faint as it was, to attend UNIBEN. As I grew older, it never became dominant, and I changed my mind to UNIPORT. Because of this though, my childhood dream of schooling outside the country came alive again. For what purpose and how this desire came to be, I can't tell. This period afforded me the opportunity to continue the search for admission outside the shores of Nigeria.

At the time, a friend of mine was a student in one of the Ukrainian Universities studying medicine. I reached out to him, and he intimated me on how to apply for admission. I did all the needful and sent all the necessary documents to him and he helped process the whole thing, saving the cost of going through a travel agent. At the same time, I made inquiries to study in Ghana. All this happened while I prepared for the JAMB exam and eventually wrote it. In all of these years and activities, one thing was constant: medicine and surgery was my undisputed choice of course to study.

My family also decided to explore another option, getting my transcript from Madonna University, since I had gone through first to third year. This would allow me to start from the third year in another University. We were willing to drop to second year, if that was what it took. So, my dad wrote and submitted another letter addressed to the Registrar, dated 23rd February, 2012.

The Registrar,

Madonna University

Okija, Onitsha-Nigeria

Elele Campus.

Sir,

APPLICATION FOR COPY OF TRANSCRIPT IN RE: IBANICHUKA, TAMUNOALA KINGSLEY, 3RD YEAR STUDENT OF MADONNA UNIVERSITY DEPARTMENT: MEDICINE AND SURGERY.

REG. NO: MD/06/646

The above-named is my son. He was admitted into the department of medicine and surgery of Madonna University, Okija, Elele Campus. He is at the end of his 3rd year in the University.

In a letter titled LETTER OF INDEFINITE SUSPENSION, with Ref. No. MU/REG/E/022 of 18th February, 2010, he was accordingly found guilty and penalized with AN INDEFINITE SUSPENSION.

From the date of the suspension to the date of this application, there has been no communication from the University on or about the student, in spite of several visits (31 times), written and oral appeals made by me on behalf of my son.

I hereby apply for a copy of the transcript of his works/performance up to February, 2010.

I shall be grateful for an early treatment.

I remain,

Yours faithfully.

Your guess is as good as the reality: no response again. This was the straw that broke the camel's back: the deal breaker for my family. The beautiful thing was that at this time, I was ready to move on and face the rest of my life, with all I had seen in the word of God from weeks of sitting under teachers of the word at WOFBI.

My JAMB result was released, and I scored 229 over 400. Not the best result for someone who wanted admission into a course as competitive as medicine. That same year, I was given admission into the Ukrainian university I applied to. Also, I made progress in my enquiries for an admission into a Ghanaian University. Though my JAMB score was low, it was fairly above 200, which was the required score to be eligible for post Unified Tertiary Matriculation Examination (Post UTME). So, I applied for post UTME, and eventually wrote the exam. When the results came out, I had a post UTME score of 69 over 100. This again was low, especially for admission into medicine. The aggregate of my JAMB and Post UTME was 64, which meant that my score to compete for admission into medicine in the University of Benin was 64.

I knew this was low, and people who knew how it worked knew it as well. The chances of getting medicine were very low. That year, about 7,000 candidates had applied for medicine. I remember checking my UNIBEN Kofa page daily, to see if I had been given admission. I checked randomly, sometimes as often as ten times a day. One evening, I was on my Kofa page when the site went off. I tried logging in again, but it was not responding. Eventually, it did respond, and I saw that I was admitted. I quickly scrolled down to see what course I had been given, and to my surprise, I was admitted into Law. How could this be? I was not an Art student, and my JAMB subjects were strictly science, for those were the requirements for medicine. I told my eldest brother, and he said, "*Maybe they are working on the site to update it, and if you are seeing Law, the chances that you have been admitted into medicine is high*". I checked a few times again, and it was the same thing: Law. Then I slept off. When I woke up early the next morning that was the first thing I checked with my phone.

As I opened the site, I saw I was still admitted. I made my way quickly to see what course, and behold- Medicine and surgery! I could not contain my excitement; I informed my family immediately. The next thing on my mind was to go print it before it probably changed again. The only thing between me and the cybercafé was our morning devotion. After that, I waited a while for the day to be bright before hitting the road. When I got to the cybercafé, I met them cleaning the office (yeah, I was that early) and was concerned that it would change to a course I did not want. Soon enough, they were done and attended to their first customer and much to my relief the course was medicine and surgery.

The joy was palpable at home. The desire to study in Ukraine and Ghana instantaneously died a natural death. All roads led to Edo State where the college of medical sciences of the great UNIBEN was calling. Monday, 5th of November 2012, clearance began, and I travelled to Edo state. I stayed with a good friend of mine whom I had met in Madonna University, one of the persons that escorted my dad and siblings to the offices they needed to visit in Madonna when we appealed for re-instatement. Having just graduated as an anatomist, he was at the time having his compulsory one-year National Youth Service program in Benin. The next day, I started my clearance but spent the rest of the year and early part of the next year squatting with my friend.

Failure Tonic 7

Failure: The new beginning.

The airplane is made to convey people in the air. But to do this, it must touchdown so passengers can board. It must also refuel. No one says to the plane, "Until you are high up in the skies, I won't board." Anyone who says this is not ready for the journey. It is not the end of the plane because it has to refuel, so why write yourself off when you are on the ground? Refuel with the right thoughts, and hit the runway again. Gather momentum and fly. It is not the end; it is a new beginning!

Great UNIBEN

My first year in UNIBEN was spent with a mixture of many feelings. On one hand, I was happy to be back on track in my pursuit of the MBBS degree; but on the other hand, I disliked the feeling of being a first-year student again, especially after going through a pre-degree, and my first to third year in Madonna.

I don't know which made me dislike first year in UNIBEN more: if it was the attitude of my classmates, which I found to be very "childish" or the fact that I had to go through the whole 'fresher' process again. Perhaps it was seeing countless 'staylites' walk into my class with one scholarship package or the other or to market a 'tested and tried' question bank for acing examinations, or a tutorial that specially had the secret to having a 5.0 GP at the end of the semester. It was so bad that I didn't spend time in class after lectures. I'd just go back to my room off-campus. I rented an apartment which one of my colleagues and friend found for me, along 'Holy Rosary' Street at Osasogie, and moved from my friend's place. It was my haven for many reasons, one of which was to hide my head, not in shame, because no one knew my past, but because it kept me from seeing too much of the first-year razzmatazz. I'm very sure most of my classmates didn't know me as a classmate in first year; for sure I didn't know many of them. I had few friends and few course mates I talked with or visited, and they visited me too.

My attitude to first year was so poor, and it reflected in my performance for I almost failed some of my courses. An "F" in any of my first-year courses would have seen me sent out of medical school. This was a rule introduced in the college of medical sciences but took effect from my set. First year took longer than was scheduled, thanks to the Academic Staff Union of Universities (ASUU)who embarked on a six-month strike. This would be my first experience of a strike—a sharp contrast to what I'd experienced in a private university and certainly not the last. I spent most of those strike seasons or breaks in Benin. I had the opportunity to look into other things that were not academic. I spent a lot of time with the founder of my fellowship, who was a senior medical student and was almost at the end of his study. He taught me much as it had to do with the gospel of Christ which was priceless to me. One other lesson I picked from our conversations was that change is constant. As he would say, *"I have seen things change for good overnight for many"*.

In my second year, I made the decision to be a part of my class; to interact with everyone instead of running home immediately after lectures. I made more friends and felt more like a student than I did in first year.

Aside from the decision to relate more with my classmates, I also changed my place of worship, which at the time was off campus to a fellowship on campus. One of the decisions I took when I arrived UNIBEN was not to attend a campus fellowship, so I joined Living Faith Church *Uwasota*, and then, they were at Technical road, but later relocated to my street at *Osasogie,* Holy Rosary Street. All through first semester of first year, a friend of mine invited me to her fellowship—Giant Stars Fellowship but I readily turned her down. Sometime in second semester however, I told her one day, "Th*is Sunday, let's attend your fellowship."* She was so happy about this, and that service would be the first that ushered me into the years I spent in Giant Stars Fellowship. This became my home and place of worship. I made new friends—many of whom became family. I grew in the word of God and in my participation in fellowship. I would eventually serve in different executive and leadership positions in the years following.

I remember an incident that took place one day in class. I had earlier heard from some of my friends in Madonna that a former lecturer in Madonna was now in UNIBEN, and that he was an Anatomy lecturer. Eventually, I met him, and we talked about how I found myself in UNIBEN. Later, in my second year, he would become one of my Anatomy lecturers. One day, he came to class, and my classmates were acting up and would not allow the lecture go on without noise. In a bid to quiet them, he told them to ask about him from me. I nearly disappeared from my seat. In my head I was like, *"Sir, these students don't know about where I'm coming from".* Immediately, all eyes fell on me. This incident fired up the rumor that this was my second degree, and after the class, a few wanted to know what degree and which school. I knew I had a mess to clear, so I told them it was back in Port Harcourt and I knew him through my brother in UNIPORT.

Some believed, but many did not. Till this day, I believe a lot of persons believe medicine was my second degree. After the class, I went to meet him in his office and explained to him that no one in UNIBEN knew about my Madonna history, and I had chosen to leave it that way. I didn't want too many questions; I didn't want anyone's expectation of me to be more than what was required. He understood my plight and did not raise the issue again, not in class or any other gathering. No one queried me again. Keeping Madonna out of the picture helped me navigate the present without being stuck in the past. I had been given a clean slate, and I was not about to trash it.

Failure Tonic 8

Failure is like a stop at Starbucks

I once had a conversation with a fair lady about failure.

I said, "One of the many stops on the way to success is failure. It's like pausing to take a cup of coffee or drink for the road."

"Like a stop at Starbucks, right?" She responded with a glimmer of understanding in her eyes.

"You get!" I grinned in approval. A stop at Starbucks can be refreshing for the road. A pause on the journey to success can be refreshing too.

THE ALMIGHTY MBBS PART 2

The study of Anatomy, Biochemistry and Physiology as a second- and third-year medical student was an out of this world experience, and made me feel like a medical doctor for real. If only I knew this was nothing compared to what was before me in every sense.

Being introduced to cadavers and dissection was everything I dreamt of when I was just a secondary school graduate and would flip through the pages of my elder sister's copy of Keith Moore's Clinically Oriented Anatomy, Ganong's Review of medical physiology and Harper's Illustrated Biochemistry textbooks. I was no longer dreaming of it; I was living it.

I loved Gross Anatomy; it came easy to me. Medical Biochemistry though abstract, I found a way to relate with, and passing it was never a problem, as every structure I committed to memory gave it away. I had a problem with Physiology, and this was evident in how I moved from one textbook to another. First it was Ganong's, then Guyton and Hall, and eventually Sembulingam (Essential of Medical Physiology). When exam was approaching, somehow, I found myself reading Guyton and Hall again.

When it was time for the MBBS part II professional examination, I was confident I would pass Anatomy and Biochemistry—at least my continuous assessment in these subjects had been good. I couldn't say same for Physiology. I was very nervous. I knew I had not done my best with it.

Long story short, I passed my Anatomy and Biochemistry with less stress and had a mountain to climb with my physiology. I remember how my physiology viva examiner used me to mop the floor (I thought I had a clue to the answer of his question, but maybe I didn't). All I wanted was to leave the viva room before I lost my breath. Eventually, the viva came to an end which marked the end of the exams. The next was to wait for the results.

If you have been around the medical school, you would know this waiting period can be very traumatic indeed. As a candidate, you would begin to remember every question asked, the toxic stuff you confidently spewed (confidence a.k.a showmanship; was everything in medical school) and the ones you aced. It's usually a time to permutate if you would hit the pass mark or not. The period was also marked with rumors of the percentage of students that had passed from the different departments. Students are left to either include or exclude themselves in the pass mark, depending on their perceived performance. In medical school, rumors concerning percentage pass in an exam are usually 90-98% true.

When the results came out, I had passed all three courses. I heard I had 50 on the dot in physiology, but I never went to check for myself. I was so happy I had scaled through without being burnt.

I was welcomed to the fourth floor of medical school by pathology and pharmacology (Path and Pharm) which was the next hurdle for us. We felt like we had arrived, as we were now clinical students. The thing about Path and Pharm is this; every senior colleague who had passed the class tries to advise you on the best way to succeed. Either we don't really listen to them or we just feel they are exaggerating. Maybe, the pressure was just inevitable.

I know every level in medical school is tedious, but Path and Pharm stands out in toughness, especially mentally. To start with, on the surface, it seems like you are taking just two courses from two departments: Pathology and Pharmacology.

The real deal is this- Pathology is made up of four different departments with four different subjects, and their block postings: Morbid Anatomy, Microbiology, Hematology and Chemical Pathology. So, in all, you have five broad subjects, including Pharmacology, which at the time had practical sessions. In addition to all these, we had to go through introductory postings in Medicine, Surgery, Obstetrics and Gynecology, and Pediatrics. I have said all these to try to paint the workload: it was massive and nothing like what we'd been exposed to in pre-clinical school.

From the time I made the decision to be a part of my class, my voice grew stronger and stronger in my class as a stakeholder—as they call it in the political arena. In addition, in 2015, I served as the secretary of the caretaker committee of the University of Benin Medical Students Association (UBEMSA) and Vice President of Giant Stars Fellowship. In 2016, I became the chairman of UBEMSA Caretaker Committee, President of Giant Stars Fellowship, and would later go on to serve two tenures till 2018. I also became a member of the school Editorial Board and later, the National Editorial Board of the Christian Medical and Dental Association (CMDA)

Nigeria – Students' arm.

At the end of 2016, a tough year of emotional turbulence, December 31st to be precise, I started my blog: diariesofhope.blogspot.com. The year ended with me in a very good place emotionally. I remember not going home that year for Christmas. I had come to realize that as a believer I am king of every circumstance, and that my emotions are under my immediate control, not the other way around. Thanks to the many messages from Joel Osteen's podcast a friend of mine gave to me. The last day of 2016 saw me take the highway to becoming all the Father had in store for me. I had prayed earlier that year that God should help me through the emotional ache, and he did. My heart desire was to know him more and be more intentional in my walk with him. This prayer was one of the quickest to manifest with answers, for the following year I made more friends that were on the same path with God. I began to be a part of life transforming meetings, where the word of God was taught in the truth of the gospel of Christ.

All these brought me to the spotlight in my class, the medical school and my fellowship. At this point, your level in school was the business of almost everyone. Without truly knowing the weight associated with this new level, everyone calls you 'Doctor'. Not passing your exams was just not an option, as it would cast a poor light on these offices, and would discourage people from serving when called upon.

Failure Tonic 9

Failure is a very productive venture to the patient

Only those who run at the sight of failure fail to see the potentials it brings with it. The more you fail, the more productive you become if you don't stop trying. Every new attempt presents a wiser you, if only you harness the good in failing by seeing where you missed it and make amends. You go again. Only this time, you have learnt the lesson that failure came to teach.

δέκα

MBBS PART III: THE FAITH DANCE.

2017 was another examination year. The MBBS part III professional examinations in Pathology and Pharmacology was here. Having been in 400 level for almost two years, all our lecturers expected us to be very much ready for the exams. For my class, the period leading to our exam was not a smooth one. As if the hustle and bustle associated with the preparation for the examination was not enough, the school management decided to renovate our hostels, and we were asked to leave our rooms to a different hostel. This was a very difficult time for my classmates, fraternizing with a new environment alongside the constant sleepless nights was so discouraging. But who cared? One thing was needful now—passing this exam.

Medics have different opinions when it comes to which class and which professional exam is the most difficult. Many go with Path and Pharm, a few with the MBBS Part IV exams (Obstetrics and Gynecology, Pediatrics and Mental health) exams. Whichever the case is, Path and Pharm is in the top two of almost every medic, not just in UNIBEN but in Nigerian medical schools.

My first experience of answering questions in categories of short and long essays was in this very class. Pharmacology would have you answer short essays and long essays under a limited time. Pathology would serve you the four OMR sheets to shade your answers to multiple choice questions (MCQ). It was your responsibility to choose which to start with, and the same was done with the theory questions.

The examinations began with the pathology courses, then pharmacology—the whole thing lasting for two weeks. First week was literally a crash program. We had the written part of the exam including the MCQs and theory sections. Till date, I have always wondered why we had to do all that in one week, when the exams could be spread into three weeks. The following week was the Viva Voce (the oral part of the exams).

The Viva part of every exam in medical school is the dread of every student. You get to face your teachers and show them if you were one of those that gave them headache while marking the written section of the exam or you made them smile with 'stuff ', or maybe you were one of those who made it easy for them, by not attempting the questions.

Perhaps in the nearest future, I will talk of the tug of war experience I had in my pathology viva. It was a bloody scene (slangs we use as medical students to describe that our lecturers bled us, like cutting an artery open and just allowing it bleed).

While I was in that viva room before my lecturers, at least four of them, I felt the comfort of God with me. I was sure I had passed Pathology.

Then came the day for Pharmacology viva. Using our serial numbers, the department shared us into different rooms, with our viva lecturers waiting for us inside. It was the normal scene during viva for students to crowd around their colleague who just finished a session like an anxious mob of press men; to ask them what they were asked and how they answered. The responses carried with them a mixed air of anxiety, tension, fear, comedy, and encouragement. After waiting outside my scheduled room, my turn came. Just before I entered the room, a classmate of mine came out and told us how it went with him and ended by telling me that the examiner, a professor who was an external examiner, was from my state, I didn't know what this was to do for me though. Somehow in their conversation, the examiner had mentioned that he is from Rivers State. This colleague of mine was from Bayelsa, a neighboring state.

Earlier that morning, I told myself I was not going to confess negatively, no matter how the viva would go, I would give God all the praise. So, I was ushered to seat down by my chaperon, a junior lecturer in the department. Before I did, I greeted my examiner and waited for him to tell me to sit down, regardless of the fact that my chaperon had earlier told me that, this is part of the showmanship associated with the medical school.

My examiner asked me to talk about Peptic ulcer disease. When asked this kind of question they want you to say everything you know about the disease and more. I started with the definition, and then I started listing the aggravating and protective factors. My examiner was just listening to me. When I was done with the aggravating factors, he stopped me and asked me if alcohol was not an aggravating factor. To be sincere, I was lost; I didn't know alcohol to be one. From the tone of his voice, I knew alcohol was an aggravating factor and I told him, "Yes, it is, and I am sorry for not mentioning it." He said to me, "You mean you don't know alcohol, *ogogoro*, (this is a popular local gin that is distilled from palm wine) causes peptic ulcer?"

His next question was, "*where are you from*?", and I said, "I am Ijaw, from Okrika in Rivers State". When I said this, he became more interested. He shared a quick gaze with my chaperon, and they turned their gaze to me. Then he continued, "*Okrika people no dey drink Ogogoro*?" and I replied in the affirmative. As I continued to talk about the treatment for Peptic ulcer disease, he looked down into the score sheet and his countenance changed, and so did our conversation.

He stopped me and said, "There is no need for this viva," and I was confused. 'No need? What do you mean?' I thought to myself. He replied almost as though he'd read my mind, "Even if I give you the highest mark from this viva, you will still not pass this exam?" At this point, I was stunned and frozen on my seat. He concluded with, "Go and prepare for the re-sit, and when you come for the re-sit, make sure you look for me". I thought I was the only one dazed but looking at my chaperone, I could see he was also lost. So, I stood up and left the room, not knowing what emotions to feel or express. Only one thing kept me sane—my resolve earlier in the morning that I would give thanks to God no matter what happened in the viva. I left the viva room with the decision that I was not going to speak negative to anyone concerning what just happened to me.

As usual, when I came outside my classmates surrounded me and they all wanted to know what I was asked and how I responded. I told them he asked me about Peptic ulcer disease and I told him all I knew. I mentioned the ogogoro part but not a word on his verdict that I had failed to them, not there and not to anyone afterwards, until the results came out.

I stayed a little with them but because I had a lot on my mind, I left the place.

I went straight to basement field (an open field with some trees in UNIBEN, where students go to pray or relax) and fell on my knees under a tree and started praying in other tongues for a while, then I did the only thing that was on my heart—thanksgiving. I gave thanks to God for bringing me to the last day of the exams and for the viva, especially my Pharmacology viva. I knew God would see me through regardless of the verdict of my examiner. While lost in tongues, the Lord told me to stand up and go look for my classmates who would need comforting due to having a tough exam. I was hesitant, "I just got here, and I am not even done with pouring my heart to you", but he urged me further to go as some of my classmates needed my attention. At this time, God had in the previous years instructed me to share daily encouragement and hopeful messages on my class WhatsApp page called "Diaries of hope", which by this time had grown into a weekly blog post.

I stood up from under the tree, refreshed, and full of joy and peace that could only be from the Holy Spirit. As I made my way out of basement field, I saw a classmate and friend of mine, and I called out to him and asked him how his viva went. The moment he started to talk, I knew he was one of those the Lord had sent me to. We both walked along the road and made our way to the school's canteen where we discussed over a meal. From the moment we met, to the time we bought our meal, and when we eventually left for the hostel, I engaged him in comforting and reassuring words. I made it clear to him he was going to pass the exams. By the time we were done talking, his countenance was full of light, and hope took over his heart. That was just the first for the day. I went on to other classmates and continued in this way of comforting them till the day the results came out. Through it all, I never lost my peace, never told anyone what happened to me inside the Pharmacology viva room.

The day it was rumored that the results would be released, I and my roommate then, who doubled as my class representative, set out to cook. Actually, he went to the departmental building (medical complex) where the results would be pasted on the notice board. I went to Anatomy gate (Anatomy gate is one of the three major gates in UNIBEN: there are stores and a mini market there) to blend melon. We were exchanging calls regarding the result; it was not yet out, and he and some classmates were waiting for it to be released. When I was done at Anatomy gate, I went back to our room, while making preparations to start cooking, my roommate called me and I said to him, "*Guy, how far?*" And he responded with a very low and defeated tone, "*Them don paste the result oh*", and I went, "*Ehen, how far na*"? His tone going lower, he said "*The thing no pure*". He was reluctant to talk, while I urged him on. He continued, "*You fail one oh*", and I was like "*which one*"? In all sincerity, I expected to hear 'Pharmacology', but then, he said 'Pathology'. I asked again to be sure I heard him and he responded in the affirmative, and right there on the phone, I told him it was nothing and expressed my gratitude to God.

When I dropped the call, I picked up my JBL Bluetooth speaker that I had inherited from my elder brother and started playing praise songs, dancing and screaming. I did it so much, that my neighbor, a final year student at the time, and one of my classmates who had passed both Pharmacology and Pathology came into the room and started dancing and celebrating with me. After a while, I knew they had no idea I failed Pathology, I paused with joy beaming on my face, and with the peace that can only be found in Christ, and told them of the situation on ground. I can still remember the puzzled looks on their faces. They were dumbfounded and didn't know what to say. They ended by saying they thought I had passed the two courses and left encouraging me that I would pass the resit exams. But they left my room with an experience that I believe took a while to sink in. Maybe they concluded I was not normal. I knew my response was not what was generally expected. However, it was every inch the only thing I knew to do then, and it was pretty much normal to me.

I informed my parents and immediately started preparing for my resit exams. My roommate took me to the then HOD of Morbid Anatomy, so we could begin plans for the resit which was slated for the next three months. The HOD was very welcoming and reassuring that if we, the resit students, applied ourselves, we would pass the exams. While we were at his office, we met a female classmate of ours. She had missed the main exams as she travelled home for a pressing matter. The Dean, school of Medicine had just given her a go ahead to write the resit exams. By the time we left the office, I was made the class representative for Pathology resit students and she was to assist me. This was the beginning of a friendship that blossomed with each passing year.

Resit classes kicked off for both Pharmacology and Pathology. We had to combine them with subspecialty postings in Radiology, Dermatology, Anesthesiology, ENT (Ear, Nose and Throat) and Orthopedics, and in most cases, prepare for the end of posting exams in these departments. It was far from an easy ride. Exam dates were fixed, and when it was time, we all went into those halls, knowing if we failed the resit, we would be repeating the class. I remember my experience during my Pathology viva for the resit exams. I wasn't fond of reading just before an exam or to gather around classmates discussing possible questions: the latter I could stomach sometimes but the former I try to stay away from as much as possible, because it wracks my nerves. So, I try to do all my reading before I go to the exam hall.

On this viva day, while waiting outside and juggling some possible questions with my classmates, I left them, took few steps towards my bag, brought out my Pathology note and with no particular topic of interest, started flipping the pages. I stopped and read through 'Sudden Infant Death Syndrome (SIDS)' also known as 'Cot death'. Before I could flip through the next topic, my matriculation number was called, and it was my time to be 'viva-ed'. I threw my note away and made my way into the room with about five lecturers including the external examiner and the HOD of Morbid Anatomy. They pointed to a seat, and as I made way to take my seat, the HOD said, "*This one has already passed*". I don't know why he said that, but that took my confidence level through the roof. I kid you not; I took the most majestic steps to my seat:

there was none like that again, in all of my stay in medical school. I literally sat down like a king. Then the external examiner was the first to ask me a question. As if my confidence was not high enough, he said, "Have you heard about Cot death?" Immediately, this took the roof of my confidence off, and it towered to the skies. What I just read before entering the room! Asides from that, the HOD of Morbid Anatomy during his revision classes with us had majored on it. With a smile on my face, I defined it, talked about the cause, the factors leading to it, the features, and how it could be prevented. The room was glowing with smiles from my lecturers and the external examiner who said that was the only question he had for me. Then, I got questions from Hematology, Chemical Pathology and Microbiology. All these I answered, but not with the same vigor and precision with which I had answered the Morbid Anatomy question. The external examiner said to me, "*I thought you would answer the other questions the way you answered mine. You can leave.*" I left the room very excited, knowing I had passed my resit exams in Pathology and was a full-fledged 500 Level student.

Failure Tonic 10

Failure is never planned for, but once it happens, get back up!

It is generally said, he who fails to plan, has planned to fail. It is clear and can be widely accepted that failure is not the primary target for men when they chase their goals. Everyone sets out to succeed, but some fail in a bid to. However, to stay down after a failed attempt is the real failure. But maintaining your focus on the goal is true success, for only then will you get back up and win the race.

Failure Tonic 11

Fear failure today; pay dearly tomorrow

Whatever you fail to overcome today out of fear will be waiting for you in the future in the same form, or must have transformed into something worse. Regret is a constant future-companion for the fearful. Failure is an arm in the school of success. To pass, you must be willing to fail, if need be, till you achieve your aim.

ἕντεκα

MBBS PART IV: THE LONG NIGHT

With 500 Level came the beauty of being a clinical student for real; with postings in Pediatrics, Obstetrics and Gynecology (Obs. and Gynae.) and Community health in the first eight weeks, termed Junior posting. Students get to rotate round these units. Senior posting followed immediately with another eight weeks each, but this time, Mental health gets to replace Community health. The exams for 500 level or 'the MBBS part IV professional exams' as it is called, comprised of Pediatrics, Obs. and Gynae. and Mental health.

We had been in medical school for many years now but this level definitely had more responsibilities than the previous ones. We got to be assigned patients from the wards, go for calls in Pediatrics and Obs. and Gynae., present cases seen in our calls the next day at morning review in the Obs. and Gynae. dept or to senior registrars or consultants, as the case may be; during ward rounds in Pediatrics.

Of all three, mental health was the most student-friendly place to be in. Maybe it's because they cared about our mental health: this is on a lighter note. You would actually look forward to being in the clinic the next day. The next best place was Obs. and Gynae. Pediatrics was so stringent; it felt like they didn't want us to be there.

New level, more responsibilities—our manuals needed to be signed daily with every activity we partook in. From lectures, to clinic, calls, procedures, patients clerked: all had a column for either a registrar's, senior registrar's or a consultant's signature. The trick was finding a balance between running after signatures and reading, which was more often than not, a tough nut to crack.

If there was any level in medical school where I lacked the motivation to learn, it was this one. Sincerely from my heart without trying to portray anyone in a bad light, there was little or no motivation in the clinic, ward round, or class rooms. Only a few took it to heart to truly inspire the students to be their best. God bless them for saving the profession, more so, my MBBS pursuit.

Whenever I went to school, I was always in a defensive mode. I expended a greater part of my energy creating a defense against the onslaught of negative and depressive words that as students we had to receive, as though it was the price we had to pay to learn. This way, I had little or no energy left to learn anything from that clinic, ward round, or class. And the cycle began again, the next day.

I don't think students should be scared of going to school. If you can't make the student better, don't make him worse than he is. Before you tag me a lazy student, ask medical students if they went through the same hurdle or not. Well, like they say, tough times never last, even though some last a little longer than expected, but tough people do. This was my case as I went through medical school, especially part IV.

About this same period in 2019, I served as the prayer secretary/prayer co-ordinator of the Christian Community on Campus (CCC) UNIBEN (the equivalent of Joint Christian Campus Fellowship-JCCF, in UNIBEN). It was a transformational period for me, spiritually and physically. I learnt a lot and grew in the process, as it was said of Jesus, "The child grew, and waxed strong in spirit, filled with wisdom: and the grace of God was upon him."

Contrary to popular opinion, serving in a leadership position was not a distraction to my academics. Rather, it was my anchor to the many troubling times I faced in school. My heart was fixed, and I knew success was sure. Regardless of what was before me, I knew failure was just part of the process. Many times I wonder how people go through school without having a community of Christian brethren. Week in and week out, I was either teaching or being taught scriptural truth that kept me.

As the exam approached, a surprise awaited my class, one that would shock many of us to our bones and change our lives and levels forever. We started hearing rumors about a new rule for the exam. These stories unsettled us and made us to seek an audience with the Dean of the School of Medicine.

What was this rumor? Well, I would start by explaining the norm and thereafter state the new rule. In UNIBEN medical school, after a professional exam, those who passed all the papers were usually to move to the next level. Those who fail one or two papers depending on the number written usually had to re-sit and pass those papers, and while they do this, are allowed to move on to the next class. This meant that they were faced with reading for the failed papers and attending classes for the new. If they passed the re-sit exams which were usually in three months following the exam in question, they continued with the new level without missing anything. I should say without missing much, because the preparations for the re-sit included remedial classes, tutorials, clinics, and its attendance requirements. So, they have an extra burden of juggling between the new level requirements and the old. However, they are allowed to resit the failed papers, regardless of the number of times. If after retaking the papers they fail it again, then they are to repeat the level and rewrite even the previous papers passed. This happens only when they have failed the re-sit exams, which is always slated for three months after the release of the last result.

The tattle which came during the exam stemmed from the Dean-Students' forum held earlier. The new rule was interpreted differently by the school and students, even though questions were asked and answered by the students and the Dean respectively. The confusion remained and germinated as the unsettling reports we received few weeks before the exams.

We heard the new rule had adjusted the re-sit structure for an exam failed. Those who were allowed to re-sit a failed exam were only those who failed just one paper, and the rest were to automatically repeat the class without a chance at re-sit. This meant that if you wrote a three-course professional exam and passed two, failing one, you were allowed to progress to the next level while you prepared and re-sat the failed paper. But if you failed two or three papers out of the three you wrote, you were to automatically repeat the class without a chance at a re-sit.

This was new, huge, and disturbing to us. Where was this coming from? Who wrote these rules? Were they aware of the heat we faced in medical school? These and many other questions we asked ourselves. We knew we couldn't go into the exam hall without trashing this matter out.

So, we made our concerns known to the Dean, school of medicine who obliged us and paid the class a visit. In the meeting, he told us what we were calling a new rule, had always been in existence, only that it had never been applied and our class was the class from which it would commence. In his words, the rules were approved to begin with us, the class of 2012.

If you remember, in 100 Level, my class was faced with a similar case, the new rule that said, “Fail one course and fail out of medicine”. That was absolutely new to the School of Medicine. Before now, if you failed a course in 100 Level, you are allowed to carry it over while you moved on to 200 Level. And now in 500 Level we were being hit with another shocker again.

To say the least, my class felt like we were the scapegoats of the medical school; the guinea pigs for every experiment.

In our conversation with the Dean, he explained that the rule of writing a resit only if you failed one paper was as old as the 100 Level rule. In fact, they were both part of a body of rules that was approved under the leadership of the then Dean of the school of Medicine, and who had become at the point of this conversation; the Provost of the College of medical sciences, to commence with our class.

Before our eyes, the exams just became ten times harder, like the biblical story of the three Hebrew boys who were thrown into a burning fire made ten times hotter for refusing to bow to King Nebuchadnezzar’s golden image. Only this time, we had just been thrown into the fire without any talks of bowing.

Our fears were palpable, our worries to the ceiling. The Dean felt it and told us to make sure we passed at least one of the three papers we are about to write, that was either Pediatrics, Obs. and Gynae., and Mental health. Meaning only those who failed the three papers would automatically repeat the class, but all who failed one or two papers would progress to the next class as those who passed all. Maybe he said these words to ease our fears. Nevertheless, those words were said and gave my class a straw of hope to hold unto if ever we were to need it.

I mean, no one goes into an exam to fail all the papers, but this is medical school we are talking about, and this was MBBS part IV. The best students had failed in the past and could fail again. It's almost as if no one is immune to failure in medical school. The reasons why people fail exams in medical school are too numerous; not to mention clinical exams: those ones are beyond the usual.

Usually, we think, "*The student did not prepare well and so, deserves to fail."*

In clinical school, you can be 100% ready and still fail.

"But, 50 is the pass mark for the exams. *Just 50!"*

I can imagine you saying that. Yes, 50 is indeed the pass mark, and it is what your best student in your secondary school is now struggling to make.

The thing we forget most times is that the students studying medicine are more often than not, the best in their secondary school days. Or at the very least, they were in the top 10 or 20 in secondary school. Now, imagine having all the best in one class; there has to be a new best.

In clinical school, the exams are divided into the written part (essays, MCQs, plus or minus OSCE), the clinical part and then the viva voce. You could score 70% in your written part and still fail the paper if you fail the clinical exam.

Yes! It has happened before and is still happening. The exam is a clinical exam, period. So, that's one of the ways students fail. And there are many other reasons, ranging from not being properly dressed; which includes your haircut or hairstyle, to the examiner transferring aggression to you from another student who in a bid to answer his questions released toxic or purulent stuff (out of point answers in medical lingo). A student may: fall ill during the exams, be having financial or emotional challenges (like the loss of a loved one) just before or during the exams, lose confidence at the sight of his examiners. All these and more can actually cause a student to fail in medical school, not necessarily because he is dull. I am of the opinion that scarcely will you find a knucklehead as a medical student. Clinical exams are the most subjective exams I have ever witnessed or even heard of.

The exams came, and we went into the halls, every one of us believing we were not that bad to fail the three papers. We would pass the three in one sitting, or in the worst-case scenario, we would pass one out of the three and still have a lifeline. True to all the stories we'd heard, the exams hit very hard, not just for me, but everyone. You would be forced to compare it with past exams. An exam that even the best students lose sleep for, and I don't mean that sort that enables you to read; but the kind that comes with soliloquizing, staring deep into space and much other weird behavior. Sometimes, a student would let out a distressed scream that would get everyone running towards them to rescue them from whatever evil had befallen them, only to meet the student with his books open before him, and maybe with no idea they just attracted everyone with such cry.

Sleep was the enemy, even when rest was highly needed. To stay awake, we resorted to all kinds of maneuvers and science. Coffee, Kolanut, Coca Cola, Energy drinks, bubble gums, stereo banging music via an earpiece or air pods, taking a stroll or dipping of legs in cold water.

After the exam, came the endless and traumatic wait for the results to be released. Not to forget the rumors surrounding pass rates, as sure as night and day, they come to pass.

Some students had the habit of leaving school immediately after the last paper, and this was therapeutic for countless reasons, rest being the primary one, and having the support at home when the results are released. On the contrary, I liked to wait till the results were released before I travelled home. And traveling home only if the holidays are long enough, which is not the case most times.

On the day the MBBS part IV professional exam result was released, I was in a gathering to celebrate the birthday of the then Chairman (President) of the Christian Community on Campus (CCC UNIBEN) with whom I served as Prayer Secretary/Coordinator at the CCC secretariat. While we were still exchanging pleasantries and putting finishing touches to the celebration, my phone beeped. I checked and saw it was a class message on WhatsApp. Opening the message, and seeing the silhouette of the yet to be downloaded pictures, my heart raced, I knew what it was; the results were out, and a classmate had generously taken a snap shot of them from the departmental notice board in order to share with the rest of the class.

Results in medical school are released in categories: those who passed all the papers—these ones are said to have satisfied the examiners, then those who failed one or two in a separate list.

I downloaded the file and quickly made it to the list of those who passed all the papers, skipping serial numbers to get to mine. I received the first shock: my Matric number was missing. I checked again and again, tracing from the Matriculation numbers close to mine only to find mine missing.

Then I moved to the category with matriculation numbers of those who failed one or two papers. That my matriculation number was there was not the shocker, but that I had failed two papers was a below-the-belt punch. I failed Pediatrics and Obstetrics and Gynecology and passed only Mental health. I froze for a moment. Immediately, my mind ran to my family and how understanding and kind they had been, they absolutely didn't deserve this. Also, I thought about the inevitable implication—I would have to repeat the class. I wouldn't be part of the final year class. But then I remembered we were asked to at least pass one paper, and that we would be allowed to re-sit the failed papers.

All the while, I was seated in silence without saying a thing to anyone. I stood up, gathered my other executives of the CCC into the one of the rooms in the secretariat and informed them of what had happened. Immediately, their countenance changed, and they tried to console and comfort me. They didn't know which one to be bothered with: if it was my failure or the fact that I was not showing any emotion equating what just happened to me.

The truth is, at this time of my life, I had come to understand some things about life. Failure is not the end. I had come to realize that the believer is king over every circumstance. Whatever I was going through was not stronger and was certainly not lord over me, and therefore I would not subject my emotions to it and react in ways that presents me as servant to anything other than Jesus Christ.

The following weeks after the release of the results were filled with more unexpected and surprising turns that would change the course of my medical school journey.

Before we could catch our breath from the result, the bells of repeating the level if you failed two or more papers out of the three courses rang again. For some of us, we'd heard from who mattered most—at least pass one paper.

And I passed Mental health, which certainly was my lifeline to a re-sit.

But the rumors grew stronger and stronger, and it became imperative to inquire from the school's authority, in this case, the Dean of medicine. My classmates chose a day, and a number of us went to his office.

I must mention here that my class had a bond so strong and enviable in medical school. We were spiritually relevant; many of us were Leaders, some Presidents, Vice presidents, General Secretaries in various Christian associations and fellowship, zealous for God. Socially, we were the life of the party in UBEMSA. Politically, we were major stakeholders in UBEMSA. You needed my class to win an election. As we approached the pinnacle of our relevance and progress in med school, politics and cliques became our weakest link and would lead to the divisions and undeclared war amongst us. At a time, the ladies were pitched against the guys in a fierce, cold and unwritten war. The cause of which was rooted in many theories and philosophies known to a few. The rest battered each other based on transferred aggressions, perceived insolence and borrowed beefs.

At the time we paid the Dean a visit, our unity was hanging by a thread. But we went all the same, to get clarity, to push our concerns and to ask that all who failed two or three papers be allowed to write the re-sit as those who failed only one. When we met the Dean, he explained that repeating the class was the reality on ground, and nothing could be done against it. Our arguments—we were not told before the exam. It was not even in the college's current prospectus, so why change the goal post when the game had already started? —all amounted to nothing.

We left the Dean's office with no change or headway in our demands.

By this time, the schedule for final year was not out yet. A few stakeholders in my class and I went to see some senior lecturers and Professors in the department if they could plead for us to be allowed to write the re-sit exam. None of these efforts yielded any fruit. At this time, the solidarity from other classmates who passed the three or failed one was still very much alive. In fact, we were thinking of not showing up for postings when the schedules were released to at least attract more attention and see if more persons could speak for us.

Soon the schedule for final year was out, and the sight of the schedule and the thought of being a doctor in the next six months began to evaporate whatever solidarity we had left as a class. Gradually, people started saying things contrary to what they had earlier stood for. Soon we were divided into pro-"resume posting" and pro-"no posting" groups, till the issue was fixed. This divide grew stronger and deeper with many unprintable words said on the class group page and under dimmed lights where only the silhouette of men and women could be appreciated.

All these changes meant one thing, a class meeting had to be called, and it was slated few days to the scheduled resumption of final year clinical postings. My classmates who had the same challenges with me, I mean all who failed two or more papers had said they wouldn't be attending the meeting as it was clear they were alone. I knew what they knew, but I opted to attend the meeting

The die was cast; majority of my classmates had jumped the solidarity ship. I was too much of an integral part of my class not to know all these. But I attended still. Not because I wanted to convince them to stand with us, not to remind them that few weeks ago, we were all classmates with one common goal—to pass MBBS part IV and head to the finish line, which was long overdue. My presence was not to remind them of how many friends we lost to the one F rule in 100 Level, or how we weathered the storm during Path and Pharm when we had to leave the hostel for another one. Not to remind them of the friendship and alliances over the years.

I went because I wanted to see it to the end. I wanted to see with my eyes the information I had and how they would play out, match faces with all I had heard. For me, it was just a necessary visit to fulfill all righteousness. So, I promised myself not to say a word but to just watch and listen, no matter what I saw or heard, regardless of who was saying what.

The meeting commenced and at first, not everyone was bold to speak their mind, but gradually, more people started speaking.

There is a saying, "*It is not what was said but how it was said that matters*". Truly, it was how the things were said and the people who said them that cut deep. I had a million reasons to stand up and say something, at least give it to one or two persons speaking from the corner of their mouths here, but I had already told myself not to make any comment.

Sitting in that meeting without saying anything will go down as one of the hardest things I did in UNIBEN. I completely put my body, especially my tongue under. At a point I was asked if I had anything to say, and I motioned no.

The summary of the decision reached was that everyone was to go and prepare for the clinical postings on Monday.

That meeting brought to fore that truly the fruit of the Holy Spirit was taking deep roots in me. I left without holding any grudge or bitterness against anyone. No transferred aggression or undoing of anyone till date and for eternity. Was I disappointed? Absolutely!

But again, they couldn't put their academics on hold—life must go on. If your dreams had a pause or was slowed down, theirs just made it to the highway.

Only a witch or wizard would be angry at the progress of others.

The tone was set—repeat it was. My family was aware and fully supportive in yet another bump on my road to the MBBS. Having a supportive family is an invaluable recipe for success.

It was time to change constituency to a lower class. Accepting the fact that I failed was easier, than actually transiting into the new class. It was like beginning a new school.

I braced myself up, and kept my eyes on the ball. This was not the goal and so, not the end.

Through the help of the Christian Medical and Dental Association of Nigeria – Students' (CMDA-Students' arm) members, and some familiar faces I knew in the class, I was able to blend in as a member of the class.

While all that was happening, the All Believers Convention (ABC, an annual teaching weekend organized by the CCC) was just by the corner. And with every ABC, there is a change of leadership to a new set of leaders, and weeks before that, the new leaders are chosen through an election, which is every inch a spiritual exercise, by the Committee of Pastors (COP).

Eligibility was guided by some rules, one of which was that final year students are not eligible to serve, as they will be graduating in the next service year.

On the day of the election, the current executive committee of which I was the prayer coordinator left the CCC secretariat for the venue of the election. Except for the Financial secretary and the public relations officer, every one of us was in our final year and not eligible to serve again. I had completely forgotten because of the change of rules that led to me repeating 500 Level that I was very much eligible. It never occurred to me. When we got to the venue and the alumni in charge of the election started reading out the guidelines, it became clear to me that I was not in final year but in 500 Level. Then I walked up to my chairman and asked him if I was eligible and he said, "I think so. Let me enquire from the alumni." He returned with the affirmative, and so, I moved over to the column of seats that had eligible candidates for the next group of leaders for the CCC.

At the end of the whole process, I was announced and so, served as the CCC Chairman for the next tenure. My friend and brother who was the former PRO became and served as the General Secretary. This would not have been possible if I was not repeating. It was a reminder that God was very much interested in my life and had not abandoned me as many might have thought. It was quite common for Christians to be given the look or even mocked openly when they fail or are going through a tough time. I thank God for supportive family and friends and for a whole community of believers that refused to see me as a failed project.

Like I earlier said, serving as a leader in any capacity puts you on the radar and makes you the focus of many conversations even when you are far from where such discussions are taking place. Sometimes, the shame and disappointment that comes with repeating a class when you are a leader in the eyes of everyone can only be experienced and not explained.

To let any of these emotions define me was to rob myself and to deny God's assurance and comfort in times like this. To say the least, I saw God in all of my valley days, and he was the prime reason why I walked tall, head and shoulders above sea level.

Failure Tonic 12

Let he who has never failed stand, for there stands a man without a destination.

It is easy to spot a man going nowhere—he is that man that has not failed at anything. This man has not attempted anything great. He is most likely a mediocre and will remain so, if he appreciates his status of, "never have I" (failed before.)

Failure Tonic 13

If failure was success, I would have been very successful

If there existed a bank that accepted failure as a legal tender, many of us would have been millionaires by now. And all those who pout would have been singing our songs of victory. If only failure was seen as a process to success, then every time I failed, I wouldn't have to hide my face in shame. I would count my returns out of every failed attempt—my successes actually—and see, that I am truly successful.

δώδεκα

THE LONG NIGHT CONTINUES

The year 2020 was an unusual year which we kicked off by writing the repeat examinations in Pediatrics, and Obstetrics and Gynecology. I had passed mental health in my first sitting, so I was exempted from writing it again. Reading for two papers was a lot easier than reading for three. Preparing for a re-sit or repeat exams in some instances come with a drag to study as at when due and this was one of the reasons people who re-sat or repeated were noticed to fail again. They try to beat the shame associated with reading what was supposed to be past. And this is not easy. Ego and pride, in most cases; stand in the way of proper preparation and so, set the re-sit students up for another failure.

For me, I noticed each time I had to re-sit an exam, I took out the first week or two to just rest from the whole anxiety and tension associated with the released result, and also take the time to plan for the next exam. I doubt if I had done more than go back to the basics each period, I had to write a re-sit.

After the first two weeks, I got down straight to studying for the next exam. I realized that my colleagues who were to repeat the same course with me, found it hard to read at this time, maybe because of the reasons I gave above. I usually get the drag like two to three weeks before the exam. I mean it happened in every one of my re-sit exams. I would suddenly lose the drive to read, but this was when every other person would be at their peak performance. This always made me look unserious, at least to myself.

I would say that as a medical student, it's good to know what works for you. As a re-sit or repeat student, the three months before your exam is not the time to copy anyone's reading pattern. I advise you take a look at yours and if need be, modify it to suit your desires to pass the exam.

2020 was the year Covid-19 hit hard on the world, and every government around the world was big on lockdown. Nigeria was not left out, for on the 30th of March, the government commenced a nationwide lockdown to prevent the spread of Covid. This led to the suspension of academic activities by tertiary institutions in the country, and as if this was not enough, the Academic Staff Union of Universities (ASUU) went on an indefinite strike.

In all of these, the 2020 National Sports Festival that was slated to be hosted by Edo State was also affected by the lockdown. UNIBEN had been renovated to serve as a camp for the athletes, and this as well, led to a compulsory holiday for all students.

Without seeing the results of our just concluded exams, we were all asked to go home. The hostels were locked and the school evacuated of both staff and students. I did not go home immediately. In fact, I did not travel until August of the same year, and the major reason was because I was serving as the CCC chairman. Another reason was this: if there was a lockdown, why move about? Wasn't interstate travel one of the major causes of the spread? And again, I had elderly parents at home, keeping them away from too much external contact in the heat of Covid was the best.

At first, we believed the results would be released regardless of the lockdown. But then, the concern of the ongoing ASUU strike added salt to injury. Waiting for our result for that long was beyond my imagination, and I believe, that of anyone. The unrest in the class was palpable and took me muting notifications from the class WhatsApp group to retain my peace and sanity.

In August, I eventually made up my mind to go home, having not been home for about a year. It's always a joy to be home. As a kid, leaving home was all one looked forward to, but as an adult, coming back home is peace. My family is a bundle of joy. My parents are always willing to have me back home. While my dad gives me the manly handshake with the widest smile and allows me time to rest, so I can resurface for him to kick start the conversation of how I have been and what was next. My mom never failed to charge towards me with the warmest bear hug that only she could give while screaming "*My pastor, my doctor!"* after which she would treat me to a savory delicacy and was ready to start the catching-up immediately.

She'd not been in her optimum state of health and was admitted in the hospital few days before I returned home. I had informed them I was coming, and they were expecting me. As I walked into the house, I saw her sitting in her favorite spot in the dining area. Her countenance brightened up with a smile immediately she saw me, but she did not run towards me or scream at the top of her voice. She was not strong, not her usual energetic self. I charged towards her and hugged her and reassured her she was going to get better.

My elder brother who had not been home since the previous year also visited home. So, it was somewhat a mini home-coming, the house was full as my siblings staying in Port Harcourt came around. I remember praying and speaking words over her again and with every opportunity to do so.

I got home on a Thursday, and on Saturday, she was not getting better so we took her to the hospital where she was seen by the doctors and was given a clean bill of health. She was scheduled for a subsequent appointment the following Thursday, which was her usual clinic day. Few hours later, she was in distress and lost consciousness. We rushed her back to the hospital. All through the way, while my brother drove, I prayed and kept praying. I called out to a spiritual mentor, and she spoke words over her and kept praying for her. I sent messages to some friends too and they joined me in prayers. When we got to the hospital, she was admitted, and the doctors did all they could to revive her. I left the ward and went outside to continue praying.

After a while my siblings came out to tell me that the doctors had gotten a pulse. Glory to Jesus! We were told she would need intensive care and since they didn't have an intensive care unit, we searched for a hospital with one. There was another shortcoming: no ambulance on ground. We were willing to carry her to the hospital in our car, but we would need the facilities that could sustain the oxygen tank and other monitoring devices she was on.

The hospital agreed to manage her through the night as she was getting a bit stable than when she was rushed in. We had family and friends on ground till about 11:00pm, and we decided that some of us had to leave so that my dad who had been calling with tears would not be troubled beyond what we could manage. So, I and others left my eldest brother and my cousin with her.

We came home and had to convince my dad that she was still alive. At home that night was me, my dad, my sister and her husband who decided to spend the night with us. Sleeping was not easy that night. I went to the sitting room and prayed for a while before I went to sleep. I had barely slept when I received a call from my eldest brother and left the room to the sitting room to pick up the call, so as not to wake my sister up. Receiving the call, I heard the saddest news in my life:

"*Kings, Amas don die.*" (Kings is what they call me at home, and Amas is what we fondly called our mom).

I froze at this message; my sister had heard my phone ring, and she looked at me with eyes that screamed, "What is happening?" I told her what our brother just said. She screamed and immediately woke her husband up. We spent the next hours trying to calm her down, at the same time trying to make sure my dad did not wake up.

By morning, we did our morning devotion without our coordinator, my mom. The previous morning, even with her poor health she had led and organized the morning devotion as she had done all my life. No one gave my dad any clue. It was hard, but we scaled through. He asked about her after the prayers, and we told him that she was doing well.

We needed the best way to break the news to my dad. It was a Sunday morning, and we decided to reach out to some senior brethren from our church who were close to him to come and break the news to him.

They came as we called and in their best moment broke the news to him. I have never seen my dad react the way he did when they gave him the news.

It was a tough time for every one of us. My mom believed in my dreams and had waited all these years to see me achieve them. She had called me "My pastor, my doctor" for years and I believe with all my heart that these very words were prophecies. I became a campus pastor, but I was yet to be a doctor. Leaving at that time was not the plan. We buried her the following month, amidst the whole Covid restrictions.

We were greatly comforted by God, brethren, family, and friends. The loss of a close one is devastating; it takes God to keep one's sanity.

Exactly two months after my mom's death, and one month after her burial, we "lost" the General Secretary of the CCC to a motor accident on his way back to school from Kwara State, the same day I was on my way back to UNIBEN. I and my executives had decided to resume immediately, as we had gotten wind of the Vice Chancellor's plans to move Fellowship activities out of classrooms, hostels and their environs. As executives, we were broken beyond words.

In every sense of it, in 2020, I was hard pressed on every side, but not crushed; perplexed, but not in despair; persecuted, but not abandoned; struck down, but not destroyed. Again, I saw God carry me through all the valley moments.

Due to my capacity as CCC chairman, I spent the rest of the year attending one meeting or the other—some with my executives. It was from one prayer meeting to another and even consultations with stakeholders within and outside the University—all these and more, to represent the fellowships and to remain on campus. All glory to God, Jehovah Jireh; the God who foresees and makes provisions; the work of God in and through the fellowships continued.

Failure Tonic 14

In failure, you're reminded of why you started.

Many times, when we set out to achieve our dreams, we can go so far that we lose sight of why we started. If we fail, it always gives us the opportunity to go back to the drawing board, and look at the reason we began the journey initially. It is like a reminder that we veered off course at a point.

δεκατρία

THE BREAK OF DAWN

In 2021, things started looking up. Covid-19 lockdown eased off gradually, and ASUU called off the strike. Furthermore, it was decided by the school management that the medical hostel would no longer be used for the National Sports Festival, so medical students were allowed to continue with their studies. The stage was set, and in February 2021, the University of Benin resumed.

Soon after we resumed, the long-awaited MBBS part IV professional results results were released and left me bewildered. I failed the two papers I wrote again: Pediatrics and Obstetrics and Gynecology. This was one time in my medical school journey that thunder struck twice. What were the odds that this could be happening to me? Thoughts ran through my head—the same I knew other friends and colleagues might have had. I had just two papers to write, and this was not my first time; I was not new to these exams, so how did I fail both of them? People who were seeing the exam for the first time and with three papers to write; passed all three.

Not again. Not after all I went through in 2020.

Some of my friends, who repeated with me, passed either all or one. This meant one thing: another repeat was looming. At this time, people had different perceptions of me:

"What went wrong; was he not reading?"

"Is all okay with him?"

"What about his family; I hope no home trouble?"

"It is definitely because he is the CCC chairman and has no time to read."

Some of these questions were out of genuine concerns, others out of curiosity, and still, others, to pick up another juicy tattle.

I knew better than to measure myself by what others thought of me, good or bad, especially bad. If not for anything, the fact that I had seen too many scenarios where the tables turned for many medical students, even those whose prognoses were worse than mine. People who failed every paper they wrote and had to repeat again and again, eventually passing all the required papers and graduating as doctors.

Change is constant, and it happens daily.

"If someone cuts branches off a tree, the tree will not die. Instead, new branches will grow. Its roots may be old. Its branches may have fallen off, and the tree may be

nearly dead. But if there is even a little water, the tree will not die." (Job 14:7-9; EASY Bible translation)

I have this life philosophy which paints an analogy using the windshield, the rear mirror and the side mirrors of a car. I say to myself: "No one driving a car forward, stays glued to the rear or side mirrors. If they ever look at them, it would be briefly and only to help the driver navigate forward."

My eyes were set on the goal, and the words I had said when I joined my current class, *"I must graduate with this class"* were propelling me, for words create the future. Without a doubt, it became tougher and biting, but I was closer to the end than the beginning. Never in the history of my MBBS pursuit, was success surer than now.

Yet another light in the tunnel was the fact that this time around, we were allowed to write the re-sit exams and still continue with postings in final year. Everyone was allowed—those who failed three, two or one. This happened without the students cajoling anyone. Only this time, failing the resit would mean repeating the class. This was the scary thing, for the class below us was too far behind us. The choice was clear: fail this resit, drop into the lower class, and go over 500 Level junior and senior postings again; write another exam in Pediatrics, Mental health, Obstetrics and Gynecology with no guarantees to pass all. The scariest thing was you got to graduate not earlier than September 2022, or you could just go the way of passing this re-sit exam (for which we were allowed to continue with final year postings) and graduate in June/July 2021. Juggling these options alone, was enough motivation to press forward.

I had no reason to give up. My family was 100% with me, never complained one day, not directly or indirectly. My friends were still very much with me, even those who were my original classmates, and by this time doctors, were every inch part of my life and medical journey. By this time my first roommate had graduated and I welcomed another. My new roommate was in the class below mine. He was heaven-sent, he blessed me with the required environment to excel as a final year student. Looking back at the roommates I had in medical school, I can boldly say, I was gifted with wonderful souls.

As my custom is, I went back to the Basics to upgrade on the things I was not doing right. To make anyone the reason why I failed was to not see the things I had done wrong or should have done better. A place I knew I had flaws was the clinical aspect of the exam. I also knew the reason this was so was the fact that I paid less attention to the rudiments. I had a difficult time as a clinical student. The motivation to learn or attend clinics was almost not present in the wards or clinics, especially in Pediatrics. The system made it easier for poor students to remain poor, if not poorer. The words and attitudes of those who were supposed to be your guides or teachers were nothing short of dehumanizing, derogatory and disheartening.

Sometimes, I tried to make excuses for them: "*Maybe they are stressed out. After all, we do not know what they are going through*". However, many of their actions were simply inhumane. Many times, they acted as if they were demigods.

The only way to jump this hurdle was to motivate yourself and to maximize the little inspiration found in the wards and clinic.

There were two senior registrars and a consultant from Pediatrics who were heaven-sent. I and some friends approached the registrars to assist us in preparing for the resit. One of the consultants in Pediatrics, who was one of the inspirations I had in clinical school gave me and another classmate of mine tutorials in his office, this lasted for some weeks before the exams. They all took time out of their busy routines to schedule tutorials for us and supply all the basics, encouragement and confidence needed to pass the resit. All these they did without making us look like idiots or less human.

I had friends from my previous and current class call me up to assist me in my preparations: from discussions to demonstrations of clinical examinations. Those who prayed with and for me played a vital role. Every loop hole was attended to.

While preparing for the exams, the posting list for final year was released. I was drafted to start with Community health, continue with Surgery, and finally to end with medicine. I was grateful for this change that allowed us to continue with final year postings, but it came with a serious responsibility, one which we were all ready to live up to. Community health posting was every inch fire and ice, choose whichever you want, you will still burn.

The University graduate is found worthy of graduation, having been groomed in character and learning. Community health definitely tests both. New every morning, was the unnerving feeling it gave. The weak and the strong cried with no shame. While the "weak" did so openly, the "strong" suffered untold misery for shedding tears covertly, only to burst into a river at home.

The expectations are usually taller than the, "*I am a final year medical student"* ego. How to go through community health posting? I would say, just be a child. I mean, don your kindergarten vest again, meet every requirement and leave in peace. Only a few battered down the door and made it through as at when due. Others who attempted it got burnt.

For a moment, I felt like having Community Health as my first final year posting was stumbling block, as it gave me less time to prepare for my resit exams in Pediatrics and Obstetrics and Gynecology. If I must be sincere, it made preparation a mountain to climb, but none the less; one that I was very much willing to climb. So, I attended my posting, knowing that the few weeks I had to spend was a season, and therefore, I put on my best behavior and clung tightly to my kindergarten vest—a humble and cheerful childlike disposition.

I later realized though that having Community Health as my first posting was a blessing in disguise. I got to do all the hard work at first, have ample time to focus on surgery and medicine postings, and harness the little extra time they come with. In all of these, my primary assignment was to pass the resit, if I was to graduate in 2021.

One of the nights when I was using the reading room in male hostel to study deep into the early hours of the next day, I could not comprehend anything; I took a stroll but it wasn't helping either. I put on my headphones to keep me alert and that also was not working. I was in a dilemma: I couldn't sleep and neither could I read. I spent hours awake doing nothing but just blankly staring into my books.

I stood up, walked to my room and lay on my bed for a while, and as I thought about what was going on, I felt tears coursing my cheeks. I allowed them flow freely. Now, I am not one to cry easily but that very moment was intense; the pressure was crushing. I allowed myself to just cry and let the steam out, after which I called my friend and classmate who had been taking me through one-on-one tutorials for the resit, to pray with and for me. He came immediately and prayed with me, after which it became easier to sleep. The next morning the pursuit continued.

Discussions began in earnest, at class level and individual level. Tutorials with the departments, the senior registrars and consultant who volunteered to prepare us also began. Continuous assessments were lined up and written and eventually, we wrote the resit exams.

I remember my experience in the Pediatrics long case. I had an infant who was rushed to the hospital after being force-fed by the mother, and presented with difficulty with breathing and cough. The baby was also on a modified Continuous Positive Airway Pressure (CPAP), this is a makeshift device connected by nasal prongs to the baby's nostrils used to deliver constant and steady oxygen at a steady pressure to assist the baby in breathing. This was a straight forward case and for me, prayers answered. I had prepared very well for Bronchopneumonia, Bronchiolitis and generally respiratory cases. At least, I believed so.

As easy as it seemed, Pediatrics has a way of taking the one by surprise. The stakes were high, and I couldn't afford to fail this exam. I started slowly and for some time, I was confused on what to do. When my time to clerk the patient was over, I was ushered into the waiting room by my chaperon to wait till my examiners were ready. The interval between the time I finished clerking and the time spent waiting for the examiners was a time to read through my work and effect any changes that were needed. Our chaperons usually walked into the rooms to verify the students attached to them and sometimes you got to know the examiners you would be facing—at least two examiners, mostly consultants. One of the senior registrars who took us on tutorials told me the names of the two consultants I would be meeting, because he knew I might shit my pants seeing the pair of them. These were senior lecturers in the department. In fact, in my first Pediatric exams, I met one of them, a professor, and it was so bloody (in medical school we say an exam or a test is bloody when the questions keep coming, and the student is not delivering the answers as expected by the examiner, either because he is blank or knows too little about it). I needed an urgent "blood transfusion" to scale through. None was administered and I was allowed to bleed till I "passed out".

So, knowing my previous history with the examiner, he encouraged me not to fret and mess the whole exam up. Words like, "*They won't eat you; they are not here to fail you, so relax and give it your best shot. It's a straight forward presentation.*"

I took deep breaths and spoke in other tongues under my breath. I definitely needed to remind myself that God was with me. As soon as they were ready, I was called to go stand beside my patient's bedside. Soon, from a distance, I started hearing their footsteps increase as they drew closer, and the voice of the chaperon telling them, "*Here is the student, Sirs.*"

My heart rate was so high; I could almost hear them audibly. My palms were sweaty and as soon as they came to the bedside and I saw them, my nerves hit the ceiling. I greeted them and took my position.

The professor noticed my nervousness, and started by calming me down, *"Relax, we are not here to harass you. This is what you have been doing daily in the wards, and we just want to hear you deliver.*" I doubt if any medical student has relaxed when told by the examiner to relax. This was quite the opposite of what happened between us in my first attempt at the exam. He started tearing me apart from a distance before he even got to me and the patient with words like, "*I hope you are done? I hope you are ready?"* It was from there to yet another slaughter (the case of a medical student who is helpless and unable to satisfy the examiner) of a medic trying to survive.

With his calming words, I started and speedily got to the end. The second examiner asked, "*Is that all?"* and I responded in the affirmative. Then questions began pouring in, from my diagnosis, to the differential diagnoses, to the patient's bedside to elicit signs. In my presentation, I had said the child was in respiratory distress. Immediately, they asked for the respiratory rate, and I remember saying what they disagreed with. They stood up, took me to the patient and asked me of the signs of respiratory distress, I started listing them, the moment I said "In-drawing of the chest wall", I was asked to show them. The Prof. pointed to the rib cage, moving his index finger over it and asked me, "*What is this*?" To which I replied, "The thorax, sir".

He responded, "W*hat?"*, and I repeated, "The thorax". He tried to be more precise with the move of his hands over the baby's ribs again, and I said "In-drawing of the chest wall". He asked me then, "What is it called?" I could not tell what he wanted to hear from me; I was practically lost, till he said, "*This is intercostal and subcostal recession.*" The moment he said it, it finally occurred to me what he wanted from me.

I was asked to examine the chest of the baby and give my findings. Next was the investigations I would carry out and how I would manage the child, and I answered. The last question was for me to counsel the mother on breastfeeding and also the dangers of forced feeding. By the time I was done, my time was over, the chaperon signaled them, and I was asked to go.

I went back to the seminar room where we were waiting for the next session, which was the Viva. In that room, something very unusual happened. I was so down and in despair—something I had never experienced for so many years. I was troubled so much I could not be consoled. My friends tried all they could to lift my spirits, but I was not buying it. Why? I was so worried about the examiners I met that I cared less about my performance and felt like it was over and they would fail me.

I carried this heaviness to the next phase of the exam, the viva which was about 10 minutes after the long case. I was so disoriented and bamboozled with thoughts about the possible outcome of the long case that I could not give my best in the viva room. Without being told, I knew I did not impress the examiners that "viva-ed" me. Carrying the excess luggage from one stage of an exam to the next is the worst thing any student can do. You will definitely destroy your chances of recovering from your flop from the previous stage. I knew this very well, yet could not help myself.

Soon, the viva was over and my countenance plunged deeper still. I could not understand my mood at this point, I am the usual "Mr. Hope"; always seeing the light in utterly dark situations. I would literally create one if I didn't see it. That day, I hit my lowest ebb. It was so glaring that my friend had to say to me, "*I have never seen you like this.*" I agreed with him, I was utterly beside myself.

I tried to stick around to see if I would catch a wind of my performance. At that point, anything, no matter how insignificant, would do. At least the general performance of the class, the percentage pass, would greatly help. Maybe if I heard the pass rate was 100%, I would know I'd scaled through.

Nothing, not even as whisper, was heard concerning the result.

I left the hospital and reached out to my friend, a former classmate, already a doctor, about how the exam went, and she tried encouraging me. It was when she started enquiring about the details of the long case and I started narrating it that I realized that I had actually answered majority of the questions I was asked accurately. The few I missed, they took time to explain it to me. Discussing with her sparked hope again in me and like a glimmer of light, I began to see God again and how I had allowed fear to have the better part of me.

Before the end of the day, news about the general performance started trickling in. Unfortunately, the success rate in Pediatrics was not 100%. However, later that day, I heard I was one of the successful candidates for Pediatrics resit while the result for Mental health and Obstetrics and Gynecology were a 100% pass.

Glory to God, this phase was done. This news was received with pomp, so much joy and celebration from all quarters. At home, it was a good day. Once again, the hurdle had been surmounted. The course was set to the finish line, and in three months, this journey would be over.

Failure Tonic 15

On the road to success, we fail many times.

Success is many things but a straight line. Like a child taking first steps encounters occasional falls, so it is with success. No one stops a child from attempting to walk just because the advent of a fall occurs while trying to stand or walk. Why then does everyone try to stop people when they fall short in achieving their goals?

This they do by mocking, badmouthing and laughing. No child stops attempting to walk after a fall, so don't stop trying because you've failed.

Failure Tonic 16

Only bad teachers put down their students when they fail.

A teacher is one who knows better than the student. He should have seen and understood that failing is not a sign of a man who doesn't want to excel. When a man fails at a thing, it means he has attempted something. It is the teacher's job to make this man see that he can try again. To abuse or put him down will amount to failing in their duty as a teacher. A good teacher, will not abuse a failing student, verbally or otherwise. In the first place, your job was to see that he passes. You either encourage him to try again or you accept you have failed him.

The worst teachers plan for their students to fail.

Failure Tonic 17

If you are yet to fail at anything, you are yet to achieve anything.

Walk up to any of your heroes and ask them if they had ever failed at anything, and you'd be shocked at the number of times they have. Some may have even failed more than they have succeeded. Most of them might speak as though they have never experienced failure, but if they would be sincere, interlaced in their success stories, are interludes of failure.

δεκατέσσερα

THE FINISH LINE

The following three months, like the last, were demanding to the very core. My belief, the energy from the victory was propelling enough to race to the finish line. I guess I underestimated the whole process—in this case, it was a dash and not a marathon. The original duration of final year is six months, and I had used the first three months to prepare and pass my resit, and even whilst attending final year postings, the priority had been to pass the resit. The time spent for the resit and final year academic burden was almost divided in an 80:20 ratio.

Again, I was pushed to the wall. The race against time was on to catch up with missed lectures and outstanding assignments. I sat for my finals, knowing I was not at my best. I lacked the confidence that came with adequate preparation. Nevertheless, I gave it my best shot. I was more in sync with Medicine, which was my last posting, in comparison to Surgery and Community health; in that exact order.

The rule is always to give your best. In the words of "The Energy god", a colleague of mine; "Keep writing as long as there is ink in your pen". And also, as "The Surgeon's hand" (another colleague) would say, "If you don't give up, God will show up".

When the results were released, I passed only Medicine and failed Surgery and Community Health. Another resit was here. However, this time, I had no reason to be troubled. Not even the fact that graduation would now be in another three months, or that my classmates would become doctors before me, moved me.

I was genuinely happy for them and myself. I only had to look back on where I was coming from to see how successful I was already in the pursuit of the MBBS. I had failed so much, I knew I was a success already; it was impossible to not graduate as a doctor now at this point.

Yes, you read that right. I counted it impossible.

Becoming a doctor was inevitable at this stage. All I needed was to do was tighten up obvious loose ends in the couple of weeks I had left, and it would be over. Going through the main final exams, I realized that the expectations most of my lecturers had were not grievous or burdensome at all. The reason I was not living up to expectations was because I did not put in the necessary work, due to the meager time I had to prepare. I was absolutely happy I passed medicine.

I gave God all the glory and assured everyone I was going to ace the resit. As my culture was, the first few weeks was to re-evaluate myself and start reading. This was easier because I knew I didn't have enough time to go through what was expected of me.

One of the reasons I passed my final year resit exam was the follow up I received from one of my lecturers who is also one of the executive leaders of CMDA Nigeria. He didn't give me any breathing space. I must say keeping up with his requirements was strenuous, but no doubt, the anchor for my study and revision. First, he had a conversation with me and other brethren from CMDA Nigeria-Students' Arm who also had a resit in Surgery, in his office. He asked that we submit the course schedule for 600 Level and a time table showing what we would read daily and the postings we would be attending. We were also to send in daily reports of our academic activities.

Reading was easy to do, because I was ready to cover every loop hole. I was not going to beg for the pass, but earn it. What gave me a tough time with his requirement of us was the postings. Not because I didn't want to attend posting, but because members of the Association of Resident Doctors (ARD) were on strike. And tutorials were majorly anchored and supervised by registrars. As if their absence was not hindering enough, all the patients in the hospital had been discharged.

To make sure we kept our daily schedule, we were also asked to submit reports to one of our chiefs in CMDA. She followed us up as much as she could, in a way that won't affect our preparations, I believe. Was I faithful to the study schedule? Yes, but the above short comings affected my attendance in clinic.

As much as I read, I also did something with some brethren that I had never done in all my medical school years. We set out time to pray, not just for ourselves, but to ask for 100% pass for everyone in Medicine, Surgery and Community health. This was not the first time I was praying for my exams. Only this time, I did something I'd never done before. In the past, the class would call for exam prayers few days before the start of the exam. And we would pray for at most an hour, and that would be all.

This time, we prayed every Tuesday, by 8:00pm. We were five in number and for over eight weeks, we held the class up before God, and he answered swiftly. At the fourth week, we received words of wisdom and knowledge; instructions to run with started coming in heavily. Before the eighth week, we were in control. We knew success was sure. In fact, we stopped praying for the exams and were praying for induction and internship placements.

Our God is indeed a prayer-answering God. He blessed our every work and expectations.

The departments were kind to us in all of the preparations, and we could see that the words the Father gave us were sure.

From continuous assessments, to the exam proper, everything was beautiful. The only exam that was close to this for me in all of medical school was my 2nd MBBS exams. The first and the last exams were the most comfortable for me. When the results were out, they were no less beautiful.

The end was finally here, and the long wait was over. The long night had finally been pierced by a blinding light which the darkness could not comprehend. The quest for MBBS degree was over.

This is my story.

This is my journey with failure.

My journey of becoming a doctor, which began in 2006 as a pre-degree student in Madonna University Elele campus, Rivers State, and was abruptly stopped in 2010 after I was indefinitely suspended in 300 Level with just few weeks to my 2nd MBBS exams and spending almost two years trying to be reinstated back to Madonna University, which was also unsuccessful was now at an end. The MB.BS was safely in the bag.

And the rest, as they say, is history.

I came, I saw—under the sun, that the race is not to the swift, nor the battle to the strong, neither yet bread to the wise, nor yet riches to men of understanding, nor yet favor to men of skill; but time and chance happeneth to them all; that he keeps in perfect peace those whose minds are stayed on him—and I conquered!

Failure Tonic 18

I have failed so much, so I know I am a success!

Each time I set out and fail to hit the mark—and trust me, I have lost count—a part of me celebrates the little victory won; I'm immediately reminded of the big picture and with a smile, I arrive at the inevitable conclusion: I am a success.

It's almost as though the more I fail at a thing, the clearer the picture of the success I seek. With each fall, I'm one piece closer to finishing the puzzle. A certain day, this dawned on me—that *I have failed so much, I know I am a success.*

Failure Tonic 19

Patience is to failure what sunlight is to a growing plant.

If a plant must grow, it needs sunlight. If one must succeed, they must appreciate the energy failure brings with it; which when harnessed properly, is a major nutrient to success.

Failure Tonic 20

Failure: a price paid for greatness

If you want to travel from a country in the western part of Europe to one in Africa, you would most likely go by air, and you would need to pay for your air ticket, except it's an all-expense paid trip, which means someone else is bearing the cost. Bottom line is, the cost is paid for you to get to your destination. Failure is one of the costs for greatness. As long as you can pay the price for success, you will definitely win. When you fail, it's not the time to quit, just know you are depositing towards success when you try

δεκαπέντε

The believer is KING over all circumstances.

The world where we live in is one filled with many uncertainties. Not to witness an unwanted situation is to not be in the world. Ups and downs, rain and tempests, turns of life that causes one to walk with a sloughed back and a downcast face, all seem to be commonplace in life.

At least, for men under the sun, offenses are a common thing. They tend to throw people off balance, beat many sore and change the course of their lives. It can be devastating.

"Then said he unto the disciples, It is impossible but that offences will come: but woe unto him, through whom they come!"

Luke 17:1 KJV

What if you can be immune to all these? And no, I don't mean how you can never have them. My offer to you is- what if you could be free from the heartbreaks and pains that come with these seasons? What if you could control your every emotion when these worries hit you down to the floor? For sure, it would be uplifting to have total control over your emotions, to stand tall in the face of the storm and to laugh when life strikes a blow below the belt.

I need you to know this: your life cannot function above what you know. What you know will either cage you or make you free. Also, understand that what you know sponsors your response to life's circumstances. How you feel, what you say, and what you do in trying times matter.

"Then said Jesus to those Jews which believed on him, If ye continue in my word, then are ye my disciples indeed;

And ye shall know the truth, and the truth shall make you free."

John 8:31-32 KJV

"My people are destroyed for lack of knowledge."

Hosea 4:6 NIV

The big question is, "What do you know?"

Let's say a world-class artist is called to draw a 2D triangle, would he be scared? No, because he draws more complex things. He is not scared because he is above such, and he knows it.

In my journey thus far on earth, and through all the storms I have experienced in my quest for the MBBS, I have come to learn the way to be above the storms of life and in control of the troubles of life when they come.

If you noticed in my story, I grew in this understanding and confidence. My knowledge of the truth has been my strength, peace and anchor. The things I know and have determined to live by are the reasons why I boldly declare:

"The believer is King over all circumstances."

Let me bring you up to speed:

BE IN CHRIST.

"For whatsoever is born of God overcometh the world:"

1 John 5:4 KJV

Not "will", not "should", but "have already" overcome the world.

Let's see other translations:

For everyone born of God overcomes the world.

1 John 5:4 NIV

Every God-begotten person conquers the world's ways.

1 John 5:4 MSG

The above scriptures are clear. If you are born of God, you are victorious over the ways of the world. The ways of the world include sin and all that comes with it: including death, offences, and tribulations, circumstances that come to wreck life, and all that will throw you off balance.

It is the exclusive right of the one that is born of God to stay victorious over every circumstance they find themselves.

Who is born or begotten of God?

Whosoever believeth that Jesus is the Christ is born of God:

1 John 5:1 KJV

Jesus Christ is the son of God that was sent into the world and through his love, he would deliver man from sin and all that it gives birth to; to give all who will believe in this love the power to live above death, sickness, pain, worries, offences, and all that is contrary to life.

To be born of God is to be born of the Spirit.

"There was a man of the Pharisees, named Nicodemus, a ruler of the Jews:

The same came to Jesus by night, and said unto him, Rabbi, we know that thou art a teacher come from God: for no man can do these miracles that thou doest, except God be with him.

Jesus answered and said unto him, Verily, verily, I say unto thee, except a man be born again, he cannot see the kingdom of God.

Nicodemus saith unto him, how can a man be born when he is old? Can he enter the second time into his mother's womb, and be born?

Jesus answered, Verily, verily, I say unto thee, except a man be born of water and of the Spirit, he cannot enter into the kingdom of God.

That which is born of the flesh is flesh; and that which is born of the Spirit is spirit."

John 3:1-6 KJV

Jesus was talking about the new birth by the Spirit of God, made available to all who believe in him.

What are they to believe about Jesus?

"For God so loved the world that he gave his only begotten Son, that whosoever believeth in him should not perish, but have everlasting life."

John 3:16; KJV

"That if thou shalt confess with thy mouth the Lord Jesus, and shalt believe in thine heart that God hath raised him from the dead, thou shalt be saved.

For with the heart man believeth unto righteousness; and with the mouth confession is made unto salvation."

Romans 10:9-10 KJV

Whosoever believes in his heart that God out of his love for mankind; sent his son Jesus to save perishing man, and will confess with his mouth the Lordship of Jesus Christ, will be saved. Born again, born of God, now a possessor of eternal life. Forgiven of all sin, delivered from sin and death, translated from the power of darkness to the kingdom of light in Christ Jesus.

"Giving thanks unto the Father, which hath made us meet to be partakers of the inheritance of the saints in light: Who hath delivered us from the power of darkness, and hath translated us into the kingdom of his dear Son: In whom we have redemption through his blood, even the forgiveness of sins".

Colossians 1:12-14 KJV

In Jesus, God came to die for man. The death of Jesus was not out of compulsion, neither because death had any power over him. He willingly laid down his life, so that through dying he would destroy death and deliver mankind that had been under bondage of death.

"Forasmuch then as the children are partakers of flesh and blood, he also himself likewise took part of the same; that through death he might destroy him that had the power of death, that is, the devil; and deliver them who through fear of death were all their lifetime subject to bondage."

Hebrews 2:14-15 KJV

"I am the good shepherd: the good shepherd giveth his life for the sheep. I am the good shepherd, and know my sheep, and am known of mine. As the Father knoweth me, even so know I the Father: and I lay down my life for the sheep. Therefore doth my Father love me, because I lay down my life, that I might take it again. No man taketh it from me, but I lay it down of myself. I have power to lay it down, and I have power to take it again. This commandment have I received of my Father."
John 10:11, 14, 15, 17 and 18; KJV

"Greater love hath no man than this; that a man lay down his life for his friends."

John 15:13; KJV

All who accept this love, receive forgiveness of sins and are delivered from sin and death. The same are now born of God and by this have overcome the world and its ways, and are victorious over all the challenges that the world will bring. No matter how tough the circumstances may be, they are above it, because they are from above, that is, in Christ Jesus.

"For the one who is from the earth belongs to the earth and speaks from the natural realm. But the One who comes from above is above everything and speaks of the highest realm of all!"

John 3:31; TPT

From this scripture, you find out that two realms or realities exist in life. And where you belong sponsors how and what you speak. It determines your disposition to life's circumstances.

As long as you live by the dictates of this earth, you come under her realities. So, it becomes common for you to go under when circumstances are not favorable. You break with every storm of life.

If you choose, on the other hand, to live by the higher reality in Christ, which is greater, you stay free from the way the natural man thinks about unfavorable circumstances. Challenges become bread for you to feast on and show the power of God in you. You literally stay above ground because of what supplies your response to life.

What you need to know is this: the truth that makes you free is that he that is from above is above all circumstances of life. He runs by a different set of rules, and is seated in a higher place than all the forces of darkness and the troubles that life brings.

"The eyes of your understanding being enlightened; that ye may know what is the hope of his calling, and what the riches of the glory of his inheritance in the saints, and what is the exceeding greatness of his power to usward who believe, according to the working of his mighty power, which he wrought in Christ, when he raised

him from the dead, and set him at his own right hand in the heavenly places, far above all principality, and power, and might, and dominion, and every name that is named, not only in this world, but also in that which is to come: and hath put all things under his feet, and gave him to be the head over all things to the church, which is his body, the fullness of him that filleth all in all.

And you hath he quickened, who were dead in trespasses and sins; wherein in time past ye walked according to the course of this world, according to the prince of the power of the air, the spirit that now worketh in the children of disobedience: Among whom also we all had our conversation in times past in the lusts of our flesh, fulfilling the desires of the flesh and of the mind; and were by nature the children of wrath, even as others. But God, who is rich in mercy, for his great love wherewith he loved us, Even when we were dead in sins, hath quickened us together with Christ, (by grace ye are saved;) And hath raised us up together, and made us sit together in heavenly places in Christ Jesus."

Ephesians 1:18-23 and 2:1-6 KJV

As a believer, you must have this understanding, that you are seated where Christ is, at the right hand of the father and far above the troubles of the world. You are an overcomer, never to be found under the control or bondage of any circumstances you find yourself. You may be in the world, but you run by a different rule, free from the effects of sin and death. Know this. It is the first step to exercising your kingship over every circumstance you find yourself in.

"I have told you these things, so that in me you may have peace. In this world you will have trouble. But take heart! I have overcome the world."

John 16:33; NIV

DO THE WORD

"Whosoever cometh to me, and heareth my sayings, and doeth them, I will shew you to whom he is like: He is like a man which built an house, and digged deep, and laid the foundation on a rock: and when the flood arose, the stream beat vehemently upon that house, and could not shake it: for it was founded upon a rock. But he that heareth, and doeth not, is like a man that without a foundation built an house upon the earth; against which the stream did beat vehemently, and immediately it fell; and the ruin of that house was great."

Luke 6:47-49; KJV

This was Jesus' teaching. What are these sayings he is talking about? It is his word, the same we have, written in the Bible; generally referred to as the scriptures.

He who hears the teachings of the scriptures and goes ahead to do them, applying them to his day-to-day living, is being described here.

He is like a man who dug deep into the ground and laid his foundation on a rock. This paints the picture of stability. First, the foundation is deep; second, it is on a rock. The strength of the foundation is the strength of the rock.

Notice, it says "when" the flood arose, the stream beat vehemently upon that house. The flood and the stream can represent the troubling circumstances of life. Using "when", means it is not conditional but a certainty that offences will come. In all of the fury of the storm, the pain, the disappointment, the shame, it says none of this could shake the house: because it was founded upon a rock.

This describes the man in Christ that does not just listen to the word but acts on it. Jesus Christ is the believer's rock. In many places in scripture, he was also referred to as the Stone or the Chief Cornerstone. Since ancient times, the cornerstone is an essential stone in the construction of the building. Its importance includes guiding the builders on how to lay other stones. It is usually the most solid of all the stones. The cornerstone is the basis for determining every measurement in the construction. Every other stone is aligned to it.

This is what building on Jesus and his words looks like. You align your life to respond as he will.

"Moreover, brethren, I would not that ye should be ignorant, how that all our fathers were under the cloud, and all passed through the sea; And were all baptized unto Moses in the cloud and in the sea; And did all eat the same spiritual meat; And did all drink the same spiritual drink: for they drank of that spiritual Rock that followed them: and that Rock was Christ."

1 Corinthians 10:1-4 KJV

The one who trusts in this stone or rock; that is the one who builds on him, will never be dismayed or lose courage.

"So this is what the Sovereign Lord says: "See, I lay a stone in Zion, a tested stone, a precious cornerstone for a sure foundation; the one who trusts will never be dismayed."

Isaiah 28:16 NIV

Peter was talking about the same stone as Isaiah. All who trust in him will never be put to shame.

For in Scripture it says:

"See, I lay a stone in Zion, a chosen and precious cornerstone, and the one who trusts

in him will never be put to shame."

1 Peter 2:6NIV

Why will the rising sea and storms of life not take down the house? Because they did not only hear the word of Jesus; they did it. Doing it shows that they chose to believe God's word even in the face of difficulties.

As a believer, your ability to stand in times of trials rests not just on the words of God you have heard but also on the ones you do.

As James would say, it is the doers of the word that are blessed or in this case; that will stand when the storms of life hit very hard and not just the hearers.

The second person described in Luke 6:47-49 is the one that hears the word and does not do it. Notice that they both heard the word, but one acted on it while the other did not.

Jesus described him as having no foundation; he builds his house on plain earth.

He did not dig deep, did not build on the rock and thus, had no stability or strength to stand the troubles of life.

These are the types that complain all day long with every little discomfort. They harbor bitterness against every other person, as they believe they don't understand what they are going through. They are angry with the Lord for not coming through and for letting them go through pain. All of these idiosyncrasies keep them blind from the help of God found in his words. Sooner or later, they begin to avoid the gathering of the saints as they don't see any reason to fellowship. Their convictions do not make it through one fifth of their trials.

They blame God for everything, forgetting that their growth is their responsibility and not God's.

"If thou faint in the day of adversity, thy strength is small."

Proverbs 24:10 KJV

Hearing the word of God taught or reading it is the first step to strength and stability. The next is found in doing it. The only reason you would fall under the weight of challenges is if your strength is small. When you don't allow God's word to dwell in you richly and to build you up, you will lack the capacity to stand tall in the day of adversity.

The believer that is properly taught the word of God, and goes ahead to do it, will never be destroyed or lost in the day of trouble. He is equipped to weather the storm. Though in the valley, he is not moved. His mentality is top of the mountain; he knows it's but a phase that he has overcome in Christ.

No matter how long the night is, he understands that joy comes in the morning. He knows the Lord is by him always, for he has promised never to leave him nor forsake him. Never the type to say God has forsaken him; he sees light in every darkness. If there is none, he will create one. Challenges, no matter how crushing they are, are bread for him. He knows how to go through the pain, knowing that God is in his midst and so, he will not be put to shame. Every word of God becomes his anchor in the tempest.

He understood Isaiah:

"But now thus saith the Lord that created thee, O Jacob, and he that formed thee, O Israel, Fear not: for I have redeemed thee, I have called thee by thy name; thou art mine. When thou passest through the waters, I will be with thee; and through the

rivers, they shall not overflow thee: when thou walkest through the fire, thou shalt not be burned; neither shall the flame kindle upon thee."

Isaiah 43:1-2 KJV

Like David, he says:

"Even when walking through the dark valley of death I will not be afraid, for you are close beside me, guarding, guiding all the way". Psalms 23:4; TLB

Like Paul, he boldly declares:

"We are troubled on every side, yet not distressed; we are perplexed, but not in despair; Persecuted, but not forsaken; cast down, but not destroyed;" 2 Corinthians 4:8-9; KJV

"I know what it is to be in need, and I know what it is to have plenty. I have learned the secret of being content in any and every situation, whether well fed or hungry, whether living in plenty or in want."

Philippians 4:12; NIV

The words of Jesus are real to him:

"And, lo, I am with you always, even unto the end of the world. Amen."

Matthew 28:20; KJV

"Peace I leave with you, my peace I give unto you: not as the world giveth, give I unto you. Let not your heart be troubled, neither let it be afraid."

John 14:27 KJV

The believer in Christ who understands all these and lives by them will never be moved; let the skies fall. I am not just saying these; I am a living testimony to this life. Since I understood my place in Christ and the provisions of God for me in his word, I have lived a stable life. In good and bad times, I know how to behave in faith. Never moved, always abiding in the peace and provisions of God. You too can, by being in Christ and trusting in him.

"Be careful for nothing; but in everything by prayer and supplication with thanksgiving, let your requests be made known unto God.

And the peace of God, which passeth all understanding, shall keep your hearts and minds through Christ Jesus."

Philippians 4:6-7KJV

These are instructions from the Bible I adhere to. I am careful for nothing, I pray about everything to God. And therefore, the attendant peace which is beyond human understanding is always with me.

I *"Rejoice in the Lord alway: and again I say, Rejoice."*

Philippians 4:4 KJV

In all these, I am bold to say, "THE BELIEVER IN CHRIST IS THE KING OF ALL CIRCUMSTANCES."

δεκαέξι

The ultimate failure companion.

Thank you for reading my story up until this point. It is my prayer that you have been able to glean a thing or two. However, I won't drop my pen without sharing with you the one who I believe is the greatest companion of all "Failures'". His name is Jesus Christ and He is the friend that sticks closer than a brother. He knows what you are going through for he is the high priest that understands fully the frailty of being human. He doesn't want you to do life alone. He wants to fully take on every burden that has bowed you down for years. He will be your anchor; help you walk on water and help you smile through every storm in life. But first, he wants to give you a new life only found in him.

Are you ready to receive his hand of friendship?

If yes, kindly say these words:

Dear God, thank you for your unfailing love towards me. I come to you broken and in despair, in need of a saviour, a redeemer and a friend. I believe you were in your son when he died for my sins. And that Jesus resurrected to make me a new man and to reconcile me to you. Jesus, I accept the life you give today and truly want to do life with you. Thank you, Lord. Amen

Congratulations, dear brother/sister!

Welcome to the family!

I would encourage you to prayerfully identify a Bible-believing church near you where you can be nurtured to maturity in your new-found faith. Also, if you were blessed by this read and would like more encouraging content, kindly subscribe to http://diariesofhope.blogspot.com where you would be edified weekly with words of hope and truth to steer you on your journey.

Kindly follow our platforms on socials

Facebook: Diaries of hope

Twitter: @diariesofhope

If you would like to reach out with feedback, testimonies from this book or for counsel and a word of prayer

Kindly send an e-mail to

Diariesofhopelive@gmail.com

Shalom

PRAISE FOR 'THE ENEMY CALLED FAILURE'

As one of those privileged to edit the book, "The Enemy Called Failure", I was really humbled by the details of Dr. Ibani's life.

Each experience he went through, and the way he was able to practically apply God's word during them, left me spellbound and appreciative of the power of God in a man's life.

Reading this book has encouraged me and made me a bit more daring. For someone who has always been quite scared of failure, the book opened my eyes to the knowledge that failure when learnt from correctly, can actually be a stepping stone to greater heights.

I'm grateful that I got a chance to be among the first who read this, and I'm assured that all who do will find encouragement and will be greatly edified.

—Miss Ofure Angela Ogbidi

TECF is a profound and excellent book which I think everyone can learn from, regardless of your experience with failure.

What stood out for me was the emphasis on the support his family gave him and how they never berated him in spite of his challenges...I think we should all take a cue from such attitude when dealing with others in their low time.

—Dr Lola Opeyemi

Author, 24.

TECF - an amazing read. It takes you through a journey, spanning about 17 years, of a man greatly helped by God. One very profound lesson from this book is the role of the family in the life of a child with many challenges. Truly, the family, by extension the home, should be the first place a child is taught that failure is not a death sentence. It is also important to note that God has made all necessary provisions for His children. God may not always deliver from the fire, but He promised to be with us even when we pass through (Isaiah 43:2)

I'll definitely recommend everyone to read through this book and learn the lessons outlined in it. Surely, you will be changed after reading.

—Dr Oshomoh, S.A

I have known a few guys who could match Ibani's grit. Ibani's staying power is mind-blowing and incredibly so. His perseverance and tenacity can't be talked about enough.

Dr Ibani was my classmate in medical school and he was one of those persons in my class that I held in high regard. I've always likened him to great men like Pastor Sam Adeyemi in his leadership style, comportment and wisdom. I wouldn't spare any words to demonstrate how much I revere him.

His book 'The Enemy Called Failure' is one of the best books I have read on this topic. I absolutely love how he connected the dots in his odyssey from an aspirer to now a full-fledged Doctor and how he redefined failure. In his words, failure is like a stop at Starbucks. It's a temporary detour, not the dead end. Failure indeed isn't the opposite of success, it's part of success!

I absolutely love the simplicity of his book and I highly recommend it. It's totally unputdownable!

—**Dr Courage Idahor**

Author, Discover it early

I met Dr Ibani in medical school, I consider myself fortunate and privileged to have been his classmate. For someone who had struggled with anxiety, he was one of the few people that understood me and I could always run to him to speak words of encouragement over me. He knew the exact words to say to reaffirm my faith. Reading through this book, I was one of the persons God told him to talk to after the MBBS part III exams i.e., path/pharm and I can now understand why I felt lighter after the conversation.

I'd recommend this book particularly for teenagers and young adults in a world where there is so much pressure to 'be successful' through worldly standards and so much unhealthy competition, this book would help to make it readers take a pause and look to God for purpose, because in the end, God always make things beautiful in his time!

—**Dr Obehi Edigin**

Spoiler alert: This book will bless you!

I count it an honour and a rare privilege to have co-laboured in the birthing of this masterpiece which you are about to read. This is not your everyday go-to self-help or feel-good-in-the-moment read, it is a living epistle of what the workings of God in a man's life.

With each page of TECF, Dr Ibani gave me the privilege of sharing an un-filtered journey with him and Daddy God. In awe of the unflinching and unconditional love of his family and his tenacious hold on God's word over his life, I have taken a key note for my own life from this amazing read: The Believer is King over all circumstances.

—**Dr Gloria Eguahon.**

The simplicity and fluency with which Dr Ibani writes is amazing. Every word used is captivating and keeps you edged to your seat till you finish reading it.

Let me warn you in advance: you'll laugh some and cry some at the stories in this book. Your perspective on how you see "The enemy called Failure" would definitely be changed for good.

—**Miss Favour Omigie**

One word comes to mind when I think about the impression that this book left on me when I first finished reading through the manuscript. The word is Transcendence. I do not look at it as a book just about failure or going through medical school or even about family, or not meeting with one's timelines. I look at it as a book that teaches one a way of being; a way of life. Ibanichuka, with his uncommon knack for sensitivity; deals artfully and quite honestly; practically, with what it means to grapple with life and to come out on top every time. It is a book about Transcendence.

I loved sitting in the classroom that The Enemy Called Failure was for me. The best part is that I get to return over and over again.

—Dr Chioma Eleje

National Editor-in-Chief CMDA (Christian Medical and Dental Association) Nigeria, Students' Arm, 2018

This book is a must-read for everyone. I won't bat an eyelid recommending it for youths and young adults. The book has changed my perspective about failure in so many ways and the story is very inspiring, I reckon that putting it to paper is such a noble task.

—Dr Orifunmishe Joshua Oreoluwa

National General Secretary CMDA (Christian Medical and Dental Association) Nigeria, Students' arm, 2020,2021

www.ingramcontent.com/pod-product-compliance
Lightning Source LLC
LaVergne TN
LVHW080815170826
845678LV00011B/2016

* 9 7 8 9 7 8 9 7 0 7 2 5 6 *